PERGAMON INSTITUTE OF ENGLISH (OXFORD)

English Language Teaching Documents

General Editor: C. J. BRUMFIT

COMMON GROUND

SHARED INTERESTS IN ESP
AND COMMUNICATION STUDIES

British Council ELT Documents published by Pergamon Press

114 *Video Applications in English Language Teaching*
115 *Teaching Literature Overseas: Language-based Approaches*
116 *Language Teaching Projects for the Third World*

Back Issues (published by The British Council but available now from Pergamon Press):

document no.	title
77/1	*Games, Simulation and Role Playing*
102	*English as an International Language*
104	*Developments in the Training of Teachers of English*
105	*The Use of Media in ELT*
106	*Team Teaching in ESP*
108	*National Syllabuses*
109	*Study Modes and Academic Development of Overseas Students*
110	*Focus on the Teacher—Communicative Approaches to Teacher Training*
111	*Issues in Language Testing*
112	*The ESP Teacher: Role, Development and Prospects*
113	*Humanistic Approaches—An Empirical View*

Special Issues and Occasional Papers

1. *The Foreign Language Learning Process*
2. *The Teaching of Comprehension*
3. *Projects in Materials Design*
4. *The Teaching of Listening Comprehension Skills*

COMMON GROUND
SHARED INTERESTS IN ESP
AND COMMUNICATION STUDIES

Edited by

RAY WILLIAMS and JOHN SWALES
University of Aston in Birmingham

JOHN KIRKMAN
University of Wales Institute of Science and Technology, Cardiff

ELT Documents 117

Published in association with
THE BRITISH COUNCIL
by
PERGAMON PRESS

Oxford · New York · Toronto · Sydney · Paris · Frankfurt

U.K.	Pergamon Press Ltd., Headington Hill Hall, Oxford OX3 0BW, England
U.S.A.	Pergamon Press Inc., Maxwell House, Fairview Park, Elmsford, New York 10523, U.S.A.
CANADA	Pergamon Press Canada Ltd., Suite 104, 150 Consumers Road, Willowdale, Ontario M2J 1P9, Canada
AUSTRALIA	Pergamon Press (Aust.) Pty. Ltd., P.O. Box 544, Potts Point, N.S.W. 2011, Australia
FRANCE	Pergamon Press SARL, 24 rue des Ecoles, 75240 Paris, Cedex 05, France
FEDERAL REPUBLIC OF GERMANY	Pergamon Press GmbH, Hammerweg 6, D-6242 Kronberg-Taunus, Federal Republic of Germany

First edition 1984

Library of Congress Cataloging in Publication Data
Main entry under title:
Common ground.
(English language teaching documents; 117)
Bibliography: p.
1. English language—Study and teaching—Congresses.
2. English language—Study and teaching—Foreign speakers—Congresses. 3. Communication—Study and teaching—Congresses. I. Williams, Ray
II. Swales, John. III. Kirkman, John (Alfred John)
PE1065.C64 1984   418′.007   83-13440

British Library Cataloguing in Publication Data
Common ground: shared interests in ESP and communication studies.—(ELT documents; 117)
1. English Language—Congresses
I. Williams, Ray. II. Swales, John.
III. Kirkman, John, 1983—. IV. British Council.
V. Series.
420   PE1072
ISBN 0-08-031055-9

Printed in Great Britain by A. Wheaton & Co. Ltd., Exeter

EDITORIAL

One of the main objectives of *ELT Documents* is to support the claim that English language teaching must be seen against the broader perspective of general education. For this reason, the current collection is of major significance, for it contains papers from a conference which explores the extent of common interest between two independent traditions: communication courses in teaching English as a mother tongue, and English for specific purposes. Not only are a number of theoretical issues highlighted by this process, but many teachers overseas will also value the descriptions of courses which have developed in Britain from a tradition quite independent from that of EFL. Such alternative approaches to similar problems are the most useful bases for self-questioning and self-evaluation.

There are in Britain many critics of the models of communication used both by teachers of English to non-native speakers and by teachers of communication to native-speakers. What has been lacking up till now has been any attempt to see how much these two traditions have in common. With the publication of these papers we shall be in a much stronger position to evaluate the strengths, and the weaknesses, of these approaches.

CJB

CONTENTS

I. OVERVIEW

**Two Halves of a Single Profession: Current Concerns of
Shared Interest in Communication Studies and ESP**   1

RAY WILLIAMS, JOHN SWALES and JOHN KIRKMAN

**Aims and Attitudes in Teaching Communication Studies and
English for Specific Purposes: the Challenge of Sociolinguistics**   9

NIKOLAS COUPLAND

II. COURSE DESIGN

**Identifying the Components of a Language Syllabus: a Problem
for Designers of Courses in ESP or Communication Studies**   15

MERIEL BLOOR

Issues in syllabus design. Needs analysis. Communicative language teaching.
On 'skills'. Language skills in a communicative event. Primary language skills.
Using a communication studies syllabus. Components of an ESP syllabus.
Major issues. Notes. References. Editor's comment.

**Teaching Higher Intellectual Skills: Why are our Courses not
More Similar?**   27

JOHN COWAN, ELSPETH BINGHAM, DEREK FORDYCE and JOHN McCARTER

Introduction. Essential characteristics of the design course. The first transfer.
Another transfer. Discussion. Common ground. Detailed comparison.
Summary. References. Editor's comment.

**Communications: the Interface between Education and
Industry**   35

MARY KING

The background to some problems at the education/industry interface. The
challenge to curriculum planning. A new approach to curriculum development: Industrial Technology and Management. The role of communications
as an integrating discipline. The education-industry interface. References.
Editor's comment.

III. APPROACHES TO THE TEACHING OF WRITING

Improving Student Writing: an Integrated Approach to Cultural Adjustment   43

BRIGID BALLARD

Introduction. The problems of cultural adjustment. Bridging the gap. Second language speakers: the double cultural shift. Conclusion. References. Editor's comment.

Writing Texts: Cohesion in Scientific and Technical Writing   55

JUSTINE COUPLAND

Introduction. The importance of textual competence in writing. The components of textual competence. Typical problems with cohesion. Improving textual competence. References. Editor's comment.

Standards of Written Expression among Undergraduates   63

PHILIP HOBSBAUM

The decline of literacy. Student writing: solecisms, analyses, fair copies. English across the curriculum. Fourteen theses. Conclusion: a place for writing. References. Editor's comment.

Research into the Structure of Introductions to Journal Articles and its Application to the Teaching of Academic Writing   77

JOHN SWALES

Introduction. Procedure. The structure of article-introductions and the signalling of moves. The article-introduction as an exercise in public relations. Applications to the teaching of academic writing. Postscript. Notes. References. Editor's comment.

Newcastle Polytechnic's Writing Centre and its Origins: a Description of an Innovation   87

CHRIS DE WINTER HEBRON

Introduction. The North American problem. Moves towards a solution. The competency-based approach. The 'trouble-shooting' approach. The problem in Britain. The Newcastle centre. Where do we go from here? The English studies connection. References. Appendix. Editor's comment.

The Writing of Theses by Speakers of English as a Foreign Language: the Results of a Case Study   99

KENNETH JAMES

Introduction. Analysis of mistakes. Mistakes which frequently led to a breakdown in meaning. Mistakes which frequently led to a blurring of the meaning. Mistakes which distracted the reader from the meaning conveyed. Conclusion. Reference. Editor's comment.

IV. EXPERIMENTS IN COLLABORATIVE TEACHING

Teaching Communication Skills and English for Academic Purposes: a Case Study of a Problem Shared   115

SMILJKA GEE, MICHAEL HUXLEY and DUSKA JOHNSON

Introduction. The civil engineering course. The language support programme for civil engineering students. Language support for 'the skidding problem'. Results and discussion. Acknowledgements. Editor's comment.

The Team Teaching of Writing Skills   127

TONY DUDLEY-EVANS

Introduction. Background. Syllabus for the course. Methodology. General considerations. Prescription. Value of team-teaching in English for occupational purposes. Conclusions. Notes. References. Editor's comment.

Team-teaching for Students of Economics: a Colombian Experience   135

BLANCA A. DE ESCORCIA

Introduction. Planning considerations. Stages of the project. Methodology. Course content. Classroom activities. Evaluation. General observations. References. Editor's comment.

V. TESTING AND EXAMINING

The Associated Examining Board's Test in English for Academic Purposes (TEAP)   145

CYRIL J. WEIR

Introduction: in pursuit of the communicative paradigm. Stage I: Who to test? Stage II: What to test? Stage III: How to test? Appendix I: Summary of difficulty and frequency data from Stage II: What to test? Appendix II: A. General introduction to session I of pilot version of TEAP. B. General introduction to session II of pilot version of TEAP. References. Editor's comment.

'Navigation Techniques' for 16+ Vocational Students: Assessment Procedures and Language Skills Development   **159**

PHYLLIS SANTAMARIA GOVE

Introduction. Current developments in communicative assessment procedures. Communicative testing in EFL. Profiling and reviewing schemes for 16+ vocational students. Analysis of language use across the curriculum. Conclusion. References. Editor's comment.

Testing Communication Studies at A-Level   **169**

DAVID NEILL

Introduction. Developments in English at home and abroad. AEB communication studies examination – an overview. Written paper 1. Paper 2. The project. Oral examination. What EFL teachers can learn from communication studies. Conclusion. Further reading. Editor's comment.

ACRONYMS USED IN THIS VOLUME

CS   Communication Skills
EAP   English for Academic Purposes
EFL   English as a Foreign Language
ESP   English for Specific Purposes
EST   English for Science and Technology
L1   First Language
L2   Second Language

I. OVERVIEW

TWO HALVES OF A SINGLE PROFESSION:
CURRENT CONCERNS OF SHARED INTEREST IN
COMMUNICATION STUDIES AND ESP

RAY WILLIAMS and JOHN SWALES

University of Aston in Birmingham

JOHN KIRKMAN

University of Wales Institute of Science and Technology

In common with many professions, teaching has become increasingly 'compartmentalized' in recent years. As a result, the first-language teaching profession has few points of day-to-day contact with foreign language teaching; English as a foreign language has become so large and self-contained that for the most part it operates independently of other modern foreign languages; and within EFL one further compartment has developed — that of English for Specific Purposes.

Such compartmentalization is both inevitable and welcome: inevitable because it reflects the inexorable 20th century move towards professionalism and specialization; welcome because it makes for more appropriate methodologies, teaching materials and research. But from another standpoint, the trend is unhealthy. Narrow and specialized professional interests tend to generate ignorance and *prima facie* rejection of course materials, methodologies and research findings from 'outside' areas. Hence the opportunity for shared professional growth is lessened, despite the fact that a little reflection and a fair measure of open-mindedness will often show more areas of overlap between compartments than might appear on the surface.

In the context of the papers in this volume, there is no doubt that L1 Communication Studies and L2 ESP are generally regarded as two separate professions. However, changing attitudes in recent years require us to reconsider this compartmentalization. After all, both fulfil a 'service role', both teach linguistic and communicative competence (but in different proportions), both predominantly teach adult professionals and tertiary-level students, and both operate to a large extent in science, technology and

1

management. We therefore hope that the years to come will see greater tolerance, greater co-operation and greater collaboration between the two. To encourage that hope, we have entitled this volume *Common Ground: Shared Interests in ESP and Communication Studies.*

At present, Communication Studies and ESP each have their own teaching materials, professional journals, associations and conferences. Although we would not want — even in the British context — to argue for full amalgamation of these structures and interest groups, we *do* wish to encourage more deliberate contact between what we regard as the two halves of a single profession, and greater awareness of each other's developments.

Why have we apparently lost contact, and what changes have brought about the need for greater examination of our common ground? When each profession first began to develop in Britain — in approximately the mid 60s — their objectives were far more divergent than they are now. The clientele of L1 Communication Studies had had a school education that stressed grammatically-acceptable sentences, well-formed paragraphs, and adherence to the conventions of punctuation and spelling. Thus CS had a firm platform to build on, and could concern itself almost exclusively with more 'macro' areas, such as the structure of a technical report, appropriacy of style for professional writing, and the formal oral presentation of information. Of course, this is still the central thrust of CS; but the English language competence of British tertiary students on entry is now more variable (see Hobsbaum, and Justine Coupland); and with the influx of much greater numbers of non-native students into English-medium institutions in the last decade, many Communication Studies Units now additionally cater for non-native needs (see Ballard, and Gee *et al.*). Also, within the ambit of Communication Studies, there is a growing demand (often from students themselves) for assistance with 'study skills' — note-making, academic reading, examination answer-writing, etc. (see de Winter Hebron). This further reflects changes in the orientation of teaching Communication Studies.

ESP began to evolve in the mid 60s in response to an awareness that certain types of learners had specialized needs that were not being sufficiently and efficiently met by wide-spectrum EFL courses. Such learners were predominantly either in tertiary education or undergoing professional training, and had much more limited and finely-focussed needs, e.g. a technician to be able to read and work from a technical manual, a medical student to read professional literature in English, a chemist to participate in an international conference. When ESP began to evolve from general English, it naturally took with it the then-current preoccupations of EFL — emphasis on linguistic competence, avoidance of error, a rigidly-graded approach to syntax and lexis etc. But (in common with EFL), ESP is now equally concerned with communicative as well as linguistic competence — as evidenced in attention to text information-structure in reading and writing (see Swales), appropriacy of style in academic writing (see James' 'Blurs'), and study skills. We no longer distinguish between categories of 'error', and we put more emphasis on the *learner's learning* than on the teacher's teaching.

We see, then, in both CS and ESP, a growing convergence of interests and concerns. Total fusion is impossible and undesirable—the needs of the clientele are different. But clearly there *are* areas of common ground, insufficiently explored as yet because of insufficient professional contact. To promote exploration of such common ground was the objective of the UWIST/SELMOUS joint conference 'Communication in English' held at the University of Aston in Birmingham in September 1982, at which these papers were presented.

Of the many themes to emerge from the conference, we should like to select just three: the need for points of access from one half of the profession to the other, the need for a sociolinguistic basis for course and syllabus design, and the need to emphasize *learning* as much as *teaching*.

By 'points of access' we mean simply that for greater contact between the two halves of the profession, it is necessary for each to know something of the other's organizational framework. Thus, the ESP practitioner needs to know of professional associations in Communication Studies, such as The Institute of Scientific and Technical Communicators (UK), and The Society for Technical Communication (USA)—with the terms 'scientific' and 'technical' being used in a very broad sense. (Addresses are given in an Appendix to this article.) Each association publishes a professional journal: *The Communicator of Scientific and Technical Information* (ITSC), and *Technical Communication* (STC). Equally important is the *Journal of Technical Writing and Communication*, published by the Baywood Publishing Co., USA. Both the ISTC and the STC hold annual conferences, as does Sheffield City Polytechnic Communication Studies Department in the UK.

In ESP, the most relevant UK professional associations in Britain are SELMOUS (the Association of Lecturers and Tutors in English for Overseas Students) and BASCELT (British Association of State Colleges in English Language Teaching)—the former catering more for the needs of university and ESP practitioners, and the latter for the local authority sector. Also relevant to the needs of ESP is the British Association for Applied Linguistics (BAAL). SELMOUS holds a conference every two years, the proceedings of which have in the past been published by the British Council as volumes in *ELT Documents* (and may be published in the future by Pergamon). BASCELT and BAAL hold annual conferences. Journals relevant to ESP are *The ESP Journal, Practical Papers, English Language Research Journal, RELC Journal, Reading in a Foreign Language, System, TESOL Quarterly, English for Specific Purposes Newsletter*, and *ESPMENA Bulletin*.

Turning to the second conference theme, we would like to emphasize the need for a sociolinguistic basis for course and syllabus design. The background to this need is that there is widespread complaint *from engineers, scientists, managers, doctors*, etc. about the quality of communication in their specialist fields. The very existence of courses in Communication Studies and ESP stems from this complaint. Such courses are not taught simply because specialists in Communication Studies or English do not like the way scientists write or speak, but because of frequently-voiced complaints from the specialist professions themselves.

But this fact presents us with a dilemma: should we, in our CS and ESP courses, teach our students to imitate the way scientists *do* communicate; or should we teach them to communicate in the way such professionals *themselves* feel would be more successful? This point has particular relevance in ESP where (until very recently) research into the characteristics of how in fact professionals write has been taken unthinkingly as the basis for course design. But such findings clearly need to be filtered through pragmatism and the wishes of the professionals (e.g. scientists) themselves.

Fortunately, there is plenty of evidence to show how to use linguistic forms in a way that will be judged more successful by the specialist professions. But we must recognize the varying pressures that make both students and teachers reluctant to aim at anything other than what *is*. Hebron's quotation in this volume from Garrison, that graduate school had a negative influence on the development of his writing skills, points to one such pressure. In academic circles, one style of writing is approved, even required; in business and industry, another style is judged 'good' or 'effective'. What models should we use for our CS and ESP courses? Many papers in this volume echo Nik Coupland's view that we should see our teaching not as a means of inculcating *the* way to communicate, but as a means of extending sociolinguistic repertoires.

But what are the pedagogical implications of such a view? We agree with Coupland that there is not enough discussion of which varieties of English should be taught. Though most teachers accept the principle of equality — that all linguistic varieties must be seen as of equal intrinsic merit — all teachers need to be realistic, and tell their students that not all varieties of English are equally acceptable in *use*. The task for teachers of both CS and ESP is to find reliable evidence to help them select which varieties to teach. We need much more evidence about the linguistic features that constitute those varieties, and about the best method(s) of helping students acquire consistency and dexterity in handling them.

The third and final theme we wish to comment on is the relationship between teaching and learning. In both halves of the profession there is a desire (more commonly felt, perhaps, in Communication Studies) that the role of the teacher should change from 'fountain-head of all knowledge/trainer' to '*primus-inter-pares*/counsellor/editor/facilitator'. This is by no means an abdication of responsibility, but a growing realization that for successful learning to take place, a learning task must be immediately meaningful *to the learner*. This in turn argues for more individual 'over-the-shoulder' editorial teaching (see James, Ballard and de Winter Hebron) and some degree of materials-input from learners themselves. In other words, we are talking of informed 'wants analysis' as being equally important as needs analysis. How such re-orientations can take place, and in what degree, is a challenge to both halves of the profession, particularly ESP. Less rigid, less pre-ordained, less neatly-packaged courses and materials strike at the heart of the tidily-organized professional edifice we have carefully built up over the years. But if we truly want our learners to acquire the linguistic and communicative skills needed in academic and professional life, then *they* must have an informed say in the nature of their learning, and in appropriate means to achieve the goals desired.

The papers in this volume were selected from some 40 contributions to the 'Communication in English' conference. The conference itself was a step towards exploring common ground between what we regard as two halves of one profession. It is our hope that teachers and materials-writers in the profession will now take further steps to explore and benefit from that common ground.

Appendix: The Organizational Framework of Communication Studies and English for Specific Purposes

1. *Communication Studies*
    1.1 *Professional Associations*
    - The Institute of Scientific and Technical Communicators
      17 Bluebridge Avenue (Hon. Secretary)
      Brookmans Park
      HATFIELD
      Herts AL9 7RY
    - The Society for Technical Communication
      815 Fifteenth Street NW (Exec. Secretary)
      WASHINGTON DC 20005
      USA

    1.2 *Journals*
    - *Journal of Technical Writing and Communication*
      Ed. Jay R. Gould
      Baywood Publishing Co.
    - *The Communicator of Scientific and Technical Information*
      (Journal of the ISTC — address above)
    - *Technical Communication*
      (Journal of the STC — address above)

2. *English for Specific Purposes*

2.1 *Professional Associations*

- SELMOUS (Association of Lecturers and Tutors in English for Overseas Students)
  1983/84 Chairman:
  Kenneth James,
  Department of Education,
  University of Manchester,
  MANCHESTER M13 9PL

- British Association for Applied Linguistics
  1983/84 Chairman:
  Christopher Brumfit,
  Department of English to Speakers of Other Languages,
  University of London Institute of Education,
  Bedford Way, LONDON WC1H 0AC

- BASCELT (British Association of State Colleges in English Language Teaching)
  1983/84 Chairman:
  Robin Davis,
  Hilderstone, St Peter's Road,
  Broadstairs, KENT.

2.2 *Journals*

- *The ESP Journal*
  Pergamon Press   Maxwell House
  Headington Hill Hall   or   Fairview Park
  OXFORD OX3 0BW   ELMSFORD NY 10523
  England   USA

- *Practical Papers in English Language Education,* and *System* (Pergamon address as above)

- *English Language Research Journal*
  English Department
  University of Birmingham
  BIRMINGHAM B15 2TT
  England

- *RELC Journal*
  SEAMEO Regional Language Centre
  RELC Building
  30 Orange Grove Road
  SINGAPORE 1025
  Republic of Singapore

- *Reading in a Foreign Language*
  Language Studies Unit
  University of Aston in Birmingham
  Gosta Green
  BIRMINGHAM B4 7ET
  England

- *TESOL Quarterly*
  202 D.C. Transit Building
  Georgetown University
  WASHINGTON D.C. 20057
  USA

- *English for Specific Purposes Newsletter*
  English Language Institute Oregon State University
  CORVALLIS
  Oregon 97331
  USA

- *ESPMENA Bulletin*
  English Language Servicing Unit
  Faculty of Arts
  University of Khartoum
  P.O. Box 321
  KHARTOUM
  Sudan

AIMS AND ATTITUDES IN TEACHING COMMUNICATION STUDIES AND ENGLISH FOR SPECIFIC PURPOSES: THE CHALLENGE OF SOCIOLINGUISTICS

Nikolas Coupland

University of Wales Institute of Science and Technology

It would be as well to start by making clear my own prejudices before considering aims and attitudes in TESP (the Teaching of English for Specific Purposes—in this case English for science and technology to non-native speakers) and CST (Communication Skills Teaching—primarily for native speakers of English, and again specifically in a science and technology context). This paper is written from the idiosyncratic point of view of someone whose primary interest is in descriptive sociolinguistics, but who has had experience of teaching both ESP and CS after a training in general linguistics. My starting point is the belief that there can be close collaboration between CS and ESP only if the two disciplines have a common, adequate conception of language. And for me, an adequate view of language has to be something like that propounded by contemporary sociolinguistics. Where the aims and attitudes of TESP and CST diverge, the differences can often be traced back to differences in the theoretical bases of the two disciplines, which may in turn stem from the characteristically different patterns of training and entry into the two areas of teaching (as discussed by Williams, 1981). My intention is not to divide, but to promote discussion: recognition of differences is often the first step towards useful collaboration.

Those who teach ESP and their CST colleagues would, I take it, accept that 'developing language skills' is an adequate preliminary characterization of what they set out to do. The aims of TESP and CST would strike an outsider as far more similar than they are different; occasionally, even insiders might not want to see their efforts as falling neatly under one label or the other. Nevertheless, we continue to talk of two disciplines and of two sets of practitioners and practices, which suggests there might be significant differences in particular aims and attitudes. But first, I want to consider a traditionally-held distinction between the aims of CST and TESP which turns out to be bogus (Figure 1).

From this model, the teacher of ESP seems committed to teaching precisely those skills that native speakers by definition possess. For second language teaching, it appears that native speakers cannot be wrong—for CST, native

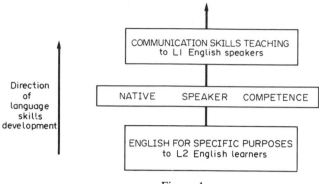

Figure 1

speakers need not necessarily be assumed even to be grammatically competent. Of course, there is some confusion here in the use of the central term 'competence' in the neutral Chomskyan sense of knowledge of one's language vs. 'competence' implying adequacy on some evaluative scale. But even more importantly, the model is based on a discredited notion of linguistic competence. As is widely recognized (and forcefully argued in Hymes, 1974), competence is inadequately defined as knowledge of grammatical rules and has to be drawn up more broadly, incorporating a wide range of *socio*linguistic communicative abilities.

To quote Wilkins (1976:11):

> "Since there will be similarities and differences between languages, the learning of communicative conventions no less than the learning of grammatical conventions has to be planned for."

As a result, 'native speaker competence' is far more difficult to specify than under the Chomskyan definition. We cannot simply set out listing the grammatical rules that an idealized native speaker 'knows'; any speaker of English needs to show awareness of what to say, in what ways, to whom, on what occasions. This in turn means that 'native speaker competence' is a fiction, because no one English speaker will be fully competent in all the communicative routines relevant to all speaking and writing situations. The self-styled 'fully competent' native speaker would find it salutary to examine the range of fields, modes and tenors that make up English stylistic varieties (Gregory and Carroll, 1978). It is not that the native speaker/non-native speaker distinction is unimportant (and I come back to this directly below), but at least there seems to be ample room for both groups of learners to develop their English communication skills by extending their sociolinguistic repertoires.

But even after rejecting the concept of the competent native speaker, we are left with the question of how much importance to attach to language as used. Does language in use constitute a target for TESP and CST equally? There is little doubt that the aims of TESP are specified (or at least specifiable) by descriptive studies of English. Applied linguists disagree about the link between particular descriptive accounts of the language and pedagogical grammars (cf. Candlin, 1973), but never challenge the basis of language teaching in linguistic description. Indeed, Candlin (1973), Widdowson (1979) and Wilkins (1974) have all explicitly recognized the need for a sociolinguistic theoretical basis for language teaching syllabuses and procedures, and sociolinguistics is firmly committed to describing and explaining everyday language varieties in use.

CS teachers, on the other hand, are less likely to be satisfied with a descriptive account and will often want to lead their students beyond 'proficiency' towards 'efficiency' in communication. CS teaching cannot be based on description if language in use is held on occasions to be inefficient or even inappropriate. To take a particular case, a descriptive account of the style of scientific and technical reports would show a high frequency of agentless passive constructions in the reporting of work done and of long compound nominal groups in descriptive sections. While the non-native English learner would be given practice in understanding and, probably, producing these forms, the CS teacher may well discourage students from using these features, according to criteria of 'accuracy', 'readability' or 'efficiency'. Different levels of prestige, then, tend to be afforded to language in use by the two disciplines, and TESP sits more comfortably than CST within the confines of sociolinguistic descriptivism. While this may seem to be a theoretical rather than a practical distinction, I feel it has some significant consequences in terms of (sometimes divisive) attitudes that are held in the two areas of teaching. Moreover, there are points at which attitudes held in both disciplines seem to conflict with those promoted by sociolinguistics. I want to consider three categories of attitudes which seem to me to differentiate CS and ESP: attitudes towards language, towards the learning task and towards the other discipline.

Alongside the canon of descriptivism, sociolinguistics asserts the principle of equality—that all linguistic varieties have to be seen as of equal intrinsic merit, despite the fact that certain varieties are viewed critically by society. (This is a claim generally made in defence of non-standard speech varieties, but the principle can be relevant in the written mode too). On the whole, teachers of English to non-native learners would, as I have suggested, accept that usage deserves if not reverence, then at least respect. But even here we find that there is little discussion of which English varieties are to be taught or of the need for L2 learners to appreciate the social meaning that attaches to non-standard forms. Taking a strong view, one could argue that consistent promotion of standard English varieties covertly reinforces received norms of correctness and acceptability. In teaching Received Pronunciation and Southern British Standard dialect forms we are leading second language learners of English to develop social personas which may not be appropriate and which may not be the ones that learners themselves, should they be aware of them, will want to project.

But it is CS teachers who, with the best of intentions, regularly have to make value-judgements about linguistic forms and are in danger of perpetuating unreasonable societal biases against 'undesirable' varieties. Clear (though fortunately rare) cases in my experience are the criticism of regional accents and dialects in spoken presentations given as part of a CS programme and the imposition of outmoded syntactic or lexical forms (of the *who/whom, due to/owing to* sort) in writing. Here, the teacher is in danger of imposing his/her own values rather than accepting a social consensus on how linguistic forms are to be used. The challenge for CS here is to find methods of developing communication skills within the framework of tolerant socio-linguistic attitudes to language, or else find convincing arguments against this position. Both disciplines need to accept the view of language as an inherently variable phenomenon at all levels (cf. Labov, 1972) and try to see the development of language skills as the development of flexibility in the handling of language rather than the inculcation of a 'pure' or 'correct' variety.

The ESP teacher may see the learning task as the acquisition of new skills, perhaps simply as acquiring the ability to perform certain communicative functions through a new medium (English). So, where there is little difference between the sociocultural aspects of the L1 and L2, the learner may already possess a sensitivity towards, say, appropriate letter-writing strategies and simply need a knowledge of the formal (English) code to enable him/her to fill out these strategies. Particularly where the sociocultural differences involved are greater, the teacher (if he/she is at all a political animal) may interpret the learning process as a liberalizing one: multilingualism promoting multiculturalism. Within sociolinguistics, the term 'additive bilingualism' has been coined (Lambert, 1974) to refer to the acquisition of a language seen as a broadening activity without prejudice to the L1, and it would be appropriate here. But this 'additive' perspective does not always guide the teaching of communication skills. The problem for CS teaching in a British context is that it is done against a background of criticism of inadequate standards of literacy and communication skills in general, even of undergraduates. In this context, it is more likely that the learning task will be viewed as exchanging one set of (inferior) skills for another (superior) set. The corresponding term from sociolinguistics would be 'subtractive bilingualism', where the motive for acquiring a new variety is precisely the original variety's perceived inadequacy.

In terms of course-design, this seemingly abstract distinction is likely to have important consequences. An 'additive' perspective is consistent with a CS programme which is a service-course in the fullest sense — a course designed to be of value and immediate relevance to students, rather than to be seen as a series of hurdles to be overcome. The 'subtractive' perspective suggests imposed remedial teaching with an emphasis on assessment and revives the spectre of traditional school English[1]. Again, there is no inevitability in this, and a broadly sociolinguistic attitude which values linguistic and cultural pluralism could guide the teaching of both ESP and CS. The obstacle is that the pluralist case is not readily accepted in contemporary British society; rather, it needs to be argued. Anyone prepared to be labelled a linguist will have experienced being asked to legislate on apparently simple questions: the correct use of . . ., the origin of . . ., the meaning of . . ., the pronunciation of . . . The pluralist, descriptivist response inevitably sounds weak and unconvincing to those asking for such clear-cut rulings. What's more, in making the response we throw away any claim we might have had to the seductive status of 'expert' — the One who knows.

At one level, then, the challenge is an everyday one for the teacher: to reconcile his/her own convictions about the intrinsic equality of diverse linguistic forms with society's (and often learners') predispositions to evaluate these forms in absolute terms: correct vs. incorrect, pure vs. corrupt. But since the underpinning of much CS teaching is the widely held feeling that standards of language use are inadequate, the more general challenge is to clarify our definitions of the terms linguistic adequacy, acceptability and correctness. This in turn may lead to different conceptions of what needs to be taught and how this might be done.

Finally, it is only right to acknowledge that practitioners in CS and ESP tend to attract characteristically different images and that these can condition the attitudes that one group holds towards the other. The long association between linguistics and the teaching of English as a foreign/second language (encapsulated for some in the term 'Applied Linguistics') guarantees that ESP teachers will be labelled as overtheoretical descriptivists and seen as members of the exclusive club of linguists. CS teachers, whose training will often have been in subjects other than linguistics or English, may be seen by their ESP colleagues as hard-nosed pragmatists with little linguistic sensitivity. Like all stereotypes, these create divides where none need exist. It is to be hoped that more face-to-face meetings between the two groups — on a day-to-day basis as well as at conferences — can show these characteristics to be overstated.

My own view is that any discipline which aims to develop language and communication skills ought to encourage its practitioners to develop at least a general awareness of language as a social phenomenon — the view articulated in sociolinguistics text-books like Bell (1976) or Hudson (1980). On the one hand, a narrow though rigorous knowledge of the formal features of English will be inadequate, as recent proponents of a communicative approach to language teaching have recognized (c.f. Brumfit and Johnson, 1979). On the other hand, the total rejection of linguistics will leave a teaching discipline without a theoretical base and lead to a confusion of aims and methods, leaving teachers to swim with the tide of social prejudices for and against language varieties. In general, the challenge for CST and TESP is to accept a sociolinguistic model of language as a basis for their aims and attitudes (as language teaching theorists have begun to do), but also to carry through sociolinguistic principles in the development of skills programmes for both native and non-native speakers.

Note

1. In my experience, these disadvantages of assessment in CST by far outweigh the advantages in terms of students' motivation pointed to by Williams (1981).

References

BELL, R. T. *Sociolinguistics: Goals, Approaches and Problems*, London: Batsford, 1976.
BRUMFIT, C. J. and JOHNSON, K. (eds.) *The Communicative Approach to Language Teaching*, Oxford: Oxford University Press, 1979.
CANDLIN, C. N. (1973) 'The status of pedagogical grammars' in Brumfit, C. J. and Johnson, K. (eds.), 1979, *op. cit.*
GREGORY, M. and CARROLL, S. *Language and Situation: Language Varieties and their Social Contexts*, Boston, Mass.: Routledge and Kegan-Paul, 1978.
HUDSON, R. A., *Sociolinguistics*, Cambridge: Cambridge University Press, 1980.
HYMES, D. *Foundations in Sociolinguistics: an Ethnographic Approach*, Philadelphia: University of Pennsylvania Press, 1974.
LABOV, W. *Sociolinguistic Patterns*, Philadelphia: University of Pennsylvania Press, 1972.
LAMBERT, W. E. 'Culture and Language as factors in learning and education,' in Aboud, F. E. and Meade, R. D. (eds.) *Cultural Factors in Learning and Education*, Bellingham: W. Washington State College, 1974.
WIDDOWSON, H. G. *Explorations in Applied Linguistics*, Oxford: Oxford University Press, 1979.
WILKINS, D. A. (1974) 'Notional syllabuses and the concept of a minimum adequate grammar', in Brumfit, C. J. and Johnson, K. (eds.) (1979), *op. cit.*
WILKINS, D. A. *Notional Syllabuses*, Oxford: Oxford University Press, 1976.
WILLIAMS, R. 'The potential benefits to the ESP profession from greater awareness of developments and practices in L1 communicative skills teaching,' in McDonough J. and French, T. (eds.), *ELT Documents 112, 'The ESP Teacher: Role, Development and Prospects,'* London: The British Council, 1981.

Editor's Comment

Nik Coupland urges us to accept a sociolinguistic basis for decisions on what to teach in both L1 and L2 classes. We should accept, he says, a social consensus on how linguistic forms are to be used. Many papers in the conference touched on this theme, but it was not extensively debated. This was unfortunate, for as Coupland himself suggests, it is difficult to establish what is meant by 'social consensus'. Does this mean what descriptive linguists say *does* happen when we speak or write in various contexts, or does it mean what the majority of language users in those contexts feel *should* happen when we speak or write in those contexts?

Coupland also encourages us to reflect on the difficulties created when special-subject departments want to include the assessment of communication skills within the general assessment of attainment for a qualification. Again, regrettably, the conference did not get down to detailed discussion of this topic. We believe that the issues raised in Coupland's paper need extensive research and discussion. We hope that publication of this selection of papers from the conference will prompt that research and discussion.

JMS

II. COURSE DESIGN

IDENTIFYING THE COMPONENTS OF A LANGUAGE SYLLABUS: A PROBLEM FOR DESIGNERS OF COURSES IN ESP OR COMMUNICATION STUDIES

MERIEL BLOOR

University of Aston in Birmingham

1. Issues in Syllabus Design

This paper raises problems and asks questions. The main questions asked are how specific a teaching syllabus needs to be and in what terms it should be expressed. The paper also addresses itself to the question of whether a syllabus devised for native speakers of a language can be appropriate for non-native speakers, and vice versa. Recent trends in Teaching English for Specific Purposes indicate borrowings from native-speaker teaching in certain areas, and, similarly, it has been suggested in more than one recent publication that the teaching of English as a foreign or second language might have contributions to make to teaching native speakers (for example, in the Report of the Glasgow University Literacy Group, 1981, and, less explicitly, in reports of the National Congress on Languages in Education). This paper proposes reasons for such developments, and some possible dangers are considered.

It is a long-held tenet of English language teaching that there are definable advantages in working to a specific syllabus, and the primary one is that, if we know what we are trying to teach, we can test to what extent we have succeeded. This allows for the subsequent revision of teaching methods, materials and/or the syllabus itself.

Classic English language syllabuses, like those of Hornby, Lado and Fries, and Mackin have been used, and adapted for use, in many countries around the world with considerable success, and many African and Asian countries have devised and revised their own syllabuses on such models. In more recent times the Council of Europe syllabus is enjoying modest success on a number of courses in different countries. Such syllabuses have been termed 'linguistic syllabuses' because they specify what is to be taught in linguistic terms. But also in recent years there is a trend, apparent most clearly in English for

Specific Purposes but not only there, to abandon the linguistic syllabus (whether it is expressed in structural or semantic form and whether or not it is confined to the sentence level) in favour of either objectives given in the form of target activities (Herbolich, 1979) or simply by specifying a set of learning tasks (Edge and Samuda, 1981).

Theoretical justification for abandoning the syllabus as we know it can be found in Newmark and Reibel (1968). They argue that the L2 learner, like the first language learner, must be exposed to "whole instances of language use" and be allowed to use the language in meaningful situations. Moreover, the language presented should be selected on the basis of situational appropriateness rather than on any other principle. Their view that "the language learning capability of the student will gradually take care of the rest" provides a justification for rejecting external organization of the elements of the language in the form of a syllabus.

A different point of view is expressed in the Report of the National Congress on Languages in Education, Working Party C, (1980). Here, the emphasis is on the "need for all branches of language teaching to ensure that their aims are carefully defined and that the relationship between these aims and classroom practice is clear if confusion among practitioners and interested parties is to be avoided". Unfortunately, the report does not go into any detail as to how these 'aims' should be expressed or even what they might be. And yet the statement is not uncontroversial since in a lot of classroom practice such definition of aims is being consciously and deliberately avoided in favour of merely providing opportunities for the language to be used. In other cases, the nature of the 'aims' is undergoing a great deal of change.

Such changes to the classic English language syllabus have been encouraged by the development of needs analysis as a tool in course planning and by the growth of the communicative language teaching movement.

2. Needs Analysis

In recent years the focus of syllabus construction in language teaching for non-native speakers has been on identifying students' needs. The work of the Council of Europe Modern Languages Project in constructing syllabuses for international use has centred on the analysis of needs (for example, Richterich and Chancerell, 1980) as has work in the teaching of English for Specific Purposes (for example, Munby, 1978).

A needs analysis may be *target-centred*, which is to say that it looks at the learners' future role(s) and attempts to specify what language skills or linguistic knowledge the learner needs in order to perform the role(s) adequately.

Alternatively, it may be *learner-centred*, which is to say that it examines what the learner can do at the commencement of the course, what problems he or she may have or what skills he may possess that will enable him to learn well in certain directions. In order to specify an adequate teaching syllabus, it is almost certainly desirable to operate both target-centred and learner-centred needs analyses.

3.   Communicative Language Teaching

A related development in second and foreign language teaching has been the emphasis on communicative goals, or, as the National Congress on Language in Education Report puts it, on the "operational command of language" with structural accuracy seen as secondary to the effective deployment of the language. The Communicative Language teaching movement has influenced syllabus design in so far as it has moved the focus away from grammatical or structural specifications and towards semantic (functional and/or notional) or situational specifications. The best-known example of this is in the BBC foreign language teaching programmes where a gradual movement can be seen away from the structural (compare, for example, *Zarabanda*, 1971, with *Digame*, 1978). In English language teaching, many new course books have been based on functional syllabuses (for example, Jones, 1977 and Blundell *et al.*, 1982). Other practitioners have focussed on methodology as the correct application of the communicative movement (Johnson, 1982, Paper 15).

In ESP particularly, the influence of the communicative language teaching movement has been on methodology, with the introduction of problem-solving techniques, simulation games and 'deep end' strategies (Johnson, 1980). Often this has by-passed the syllabus in the sense that the need for communication in the classroom has been seen to be the paramount objective. Thus teachers have introduced games into the classroom as an end in themselves without concern as to the precise specification of what is being taught or practised, in the belief that the activity itself is justified psycholinguistically.

One result of the influence of needs analysis and the Communicative Language Teaching movement has been to move foreign language syllabuses and communication studies syllabuses closer together. The syllabus for *General and Communication Studies*, produced by the Technician Education Council Specialist Panel II 1981, looks very similar in places to some ESP syllabuses. Presented in the form of behavioural objectives ('learning outcomes'), it includes 'pure' communicative activities (for example, Section 3, 'Communicates Effectively by Telephone') as well as activities related to specific subject content (for example, Section 1.4 'states his/her rights and obligations in relation to injury, sickness and safety').

Williams (1981) has already identified some common areas of interest in ESP and Communication Studies courses in universities, and fruitful cross-fertilization is taking place. Nevertheless, in course design there are issues which need to be clarified if there is to be further close identification of these groups.

4. On 'Skills'

Many approaches to syllabus construction focus on skills, but, since the term 'skill' is used in a number of different ways in English language teaching, it is important to clarify these uses before further discussion is possible. In Communication Studies, reference is made to less specifically language-referenced skills such as 'intellectual skills' and 'thinking skills' (as, for example, in the Technician Education Council syllabus mentioned above). But, even if we exclude these, four uses of the term are still currently found in language teaching literature[1]:

1. For many years it has been customary to refer to the 'four skills', meaning simply *listening, speaking, reading* and *writing*, and, although this division has been criticised as 'superficial' (Corder, 1973) and 'inadequate' (Munby, 1978), its use has survived effectively into recent times as a basis for certain types of syllabus (Robinson, 1980). Often, of course, the four-way split is only a starting point for more complex categorization of mode of the type considered by Gregory (1967).

2. In addition, it has become usual to use the word 'skill' to refer to such components of a syllabus as 'using the telephone' or 'writing business reports'. This use differs from that in (1) since the skills are always situation-specific or genre-specific. Munby (1978) distinguishes these from language skills and prefers the term 'activity', but in native-speaker teaching 'skill' is also used in this way.

3. Yet another use of 'skills' is in the syllabus component 'study skills'. 'Study skills' are such activities as 'note making' or 'using the dictionary', and are those support activities which enable learners to learn other subjects more effectively. Skills of this type are different from those described under (2) since they cannot be seen as target activities.

4. The final use of the term 'skill', and the one which is considered in more detail in this paper, is that used by Munby (1978). He classifies what he calls 'language skills' into a taxonomy of 260 micro-skills (in 54 groups) for the purpose of selection of appropriate skills for inclusion in syllabuses of English for Specific Purposes. The selected skills, together with a selection of micro-functions, are claimed to be 'enabling factors' for activities. He gives as an example the case that a reader needs to be able to understand "relations between parts of a text through the grammatical cohesion device of logical connectors" (a language skill) in order to be able to read and understand a text (a communicative activity). Munby's use of the term 'skills' is in one sense narrow since it excludes the

performance of activities, and in another sense extremely wide since it includes the whole range of language activities from the understanding of phonemic contrast to the transcoding of information.

5. Language Skills in a Communicative Event

Munby's list of language skills is of interest in the context of this paper because in the list he includes those skills required, he claims, for the realisation of performance in a communicative event. Munby does not, in this list, make any distinction between those skills which we might reasonably expect a native speaker to acquire regardless of the education system, and those which he or she learns as a *result* of the education system. It is implicit in Munby's presentation that the skills he lists are all considered as possible components of a non-native speaker syllabus (from which a selection is made for any given syllabus on the basis of learner needs), and yet only a small proportion of these skills are taught explicitly to native speakers. To take specific examples, the skills in Group 1 (discriminating sounds in isolate word forms) are skills that society expects the native speaker to acquire outside the classroom, whereas the skills in Group 44 (basic reference skills) are clearly skills that are often taught within the education system. 'Manipulating the script of the language: forming the graphemes' (Skill 18.1) forms as much a part of the native-speaker school language syllabus (albeit usually at a very early age) as it does the L2 syllabus, whereas 'Expressing attitudinal meaning through pitch height' is not normally taught to native speakers.

There are, however, areas where such distinctions are not so clear. Take, for example, Skill 23:
    Understanding information in the text, not explicitly stated, through
    1. making inferences
    2. understanding figurative language.

Most native English speakers of 8 or 9 years of age can make inferences about the moral behaviour of characters in a comic and understand the figurative language of common proverbs and sayings, but much of the traditional language education of native speakers concerns the extension of such skills to different fields and to more mature texts. Most native speakers have some control of Skill 25.1 ('Expressing conceptual meaning: quantity and amount') and can ask for a pound of plums at the greengrocers, but they nevertheless depend on the education system for instruction on expression of chemical weights.

The same type of confusion arises when we consider Skill 29, 'Expressing relations within the sentence'. At one level, since the adult native speaker has command of the language and can use sentences of English grammatically with the correct word order, he clearly has this skill. Nevertheless, occasions occur where it apparently breaks down, particularly with the written language. An interesting recent description of such breakdown appeared recently in the Report of the Glasgow Literacy Group[2]. Many examples from this report testify to native speakers whose written English requires explicit instruction in expressing relations within the sentence.

Table 1 attempts to specify the skills used by native speakers in a communicative event. These I have divided into two columns: in the first column are the skills acquired naturally, and in the second are those normally taught (but not always learned) in the education system. Where these skills seem to be similar to those listed by Munby in his taxonomy of language skills, I have indicated this on the table by 'TLS' (Taxonomy of Language Skills). The overlap suggested above is shown in this way. Thus in H, the same TLS skills come in both columns since any of these skills might be acquired naturally (as in conversation, joke-telling, etc.) or in a formal language or communication studies course (as in the taking of minutes, oral presentations, etc.).

There is, of course, no suggestion that this list is ordered in any way. The native speaker does not fully acquire the sound system of the language (Section A) before he starts to acquire the grammatical rules. The child appears to learn everything at once: discourse structure, intonation, phonemes, grammar, knowledge of the world, and so on. Moreover, we do not know when the ability to acquire language skills ceases, if at all. It seems likely that we can go on acquiring such skills until the end of our lives. Writers, for example, acquire new vocabulary and use old vocabulary in new ways. Hence no assumptions are made about *how* native speakers gain control of the skills listed in Column 2. It may well be that the innate mechanisms that enable us to acquire the skills in Column 1 are those also activated for the skills in Column 2. The difference is that the language skills in Column 2 are, for some reason, the 'property' of the education system, of the body of knowledge valued and taught by our society: those in Column 1 are part of the nature of human communication.

6. Primary Language Skills

Self-evidently, non-native speakers cannot perform Column 1 skills in the target language before they begin to learn that language, whether or not they can perform them in their own language. Thus, while it is not expected that Column 1 skills A, B, E, for example, would normally appear in a native-speaker Communication Studies syllabus, they might need to appear in a syllabus for non-native speakers. It does seem the case, however, that certain enabling skills associated with first language use (Summary Skills, for example) are transferable in part to the target language, particularly where sociocultural aspects of the two languages are similar[3], and this factor may modify the inclusion of such skills in a syllabus. At one time it was widely thought to be the case that since speech was the primary language skill, good language courses should provide initial teaching in listening and speaking. This view is no longer popular, particularly in ESP, and it is normal in some

TABLE 1. *Native Speaker Language Skills*

	SKILLS ACQUIRED NATURALLY	*SKILLS TAUGHT IN THE EDUCATION SYSTEM (CULTURALLY ACQUIRED)*
A	*Sound discrimination and articulation of L—phonetics, phonology, intonation, pause, tempo (TLS* 1 to 16)*	*Conventional articulation for very specific purposes, e.g. speech making, drama, etc.*
B	*Operation of grammatical rules of L—syntax, morphology, lexical and relational rules (TLS 28 to 29)*	
C		*Writing system (graphemes), reading and writing, spelling. (TLS 17 to 18)*
D		*Conventions of written 'grammar': punctuation, capitalization, written sentence structures and morphology.*
E	*Use of lexis*	*Use of lexis of specific varieties (terminology, academic vocabulary, etc.)*
F		*Formal word formation—stems, roots, derivations, prefixes, suffixes, etc. (TLS 19)*
G	*Operation of elements of discourse—in conversation and specific oral conventions (TLS 35 to 39 and 47 to 50 in part)*	*Operation of elements of discourse function—specific written conventions (TLS 35 to 39 and 47 to 50 in part)*
H	*Summary skills (TLS 37 to 43 in part)*	*Summary skills (TLS 37 to 43 in part)*
I	*Recording and relaying information (TLS 53 to 54)*	*Recording and relaying information (TLS 53 to 54)*
J	*Operation of cohesive relationships in L: lexical and grammatical cohesion—repetition, collocation, reference, etc. (TLS 30 to 35)*	*Operation of cohesive relationships in L (TLS 30 to 35)*
K	*Operation of pragmatics: the relationships possible between L and the real world: exophoric reference, mutual knowledge, etc. (TLS 34)*	*Operation of pragmatics*
L		*Reference skills: use of dictionaires, libraries, etc.[4] (TLS 44)*
M		*Conventions of written layout or format for various specific genres (TLS 44.1)*
N		*Reading skills: skimming, scanning, etc. (TLS 45 to 46)*
O		*Information transfer (TLS 51 to 52)*
P	*Operation of semiotic systems in L: certain narrative systems, popular metaphor, folk myth, proverb, idiom, etc.*	*Operation of semiotic systems in L: certain narrative systems, metaphor, scientific models, codes, etc.*

*TLS Taxonomy of Language Skills (Munby, 1978)

countries to teach, for example, only a library use of English for reference and reading purposes to students who do not know the spoken language. In ESP we frequently find situations where priorities of this type are important because of shortage of time. But very little is really understood about the relationship of the skills in Column 1 to those in Column 2. It might well be the case, for example, that the native speaker who, for one reason or another, has highly-developed skills in recording and relaying information in natural situations (carrying messages from mother to school, or explaining instructions to younger siblings) is also more likely to perform effectively in more formal acts of recoding and relaying information, like taking and relaying telephone messages (TEC 1981, 3.3). We do not know, however, whether the non-native speaker who by-passes the Column 1 skills is disadvantaged as a language learner, or whether he is somehow compensated by his first language skills.

7. Using a Communication Studies Syllabus

What is clear is that TEC-type syllabuses, which are designed for students who have a command not only of Column 1 skills but also of many of those listed in Column 2, cannot easily be transferred directly to courses for non-native speakers. Such syllabuses provide objectives, many expressed as communicative activities for events involving (to use Munby's terminology) participant identity, setting, interaction, and so on; but they are not linguistic syllabuses in the sense that they do not specify language skills or language functions.

An interesting experiment is currently taking place at the Royal Guard Boys' Technical School in Oman, where, under the auspices of Bradford College, students are working towards a TEC Diploma in Electronics and Instrumentation which includes the unit *General and Communicative Studies*. Although the Technician Education Council has still to approve the scheme, the syllabus is in use at present. Jonathan Elliman (personal communication), who is the department head in charge of implementing the Communications programmes, writes: "the objectives state what the student has to do, not what features of language the student must be able to handle in order to realize these objectives . . . In an EFL/ESP situation, such a syllabus needs a whole pre-factum syllabus underlying it expressed in linguistic terms (language skills, functions, forms, vocabulary, sound and handwriting systems, what-have-you.)"

Thus it appears that additional elements in some form are necessary for the successful use of this type of syllabus with non-native speakers.

8. Components of an ESP Syllabus

It has already been pointed out that the ESP syllabus differs from the traditional ELT syllabus in the emphasis given to needs analysis. But the specification of language skills in terms of those informally acquired as opposed to those formally learned indicates another difference. Traditionally the primary task of the L2 language class was to teach those skills in Column 1 ('the language') and the secondary task was to teach certain cultural manifestations such as those skills given in Column 2 (like formal word formation, or 'skimming'). In ESP, selections are made from both columns as needs dictate.

The view of Newmark and Reibel (1968) concerning the learner's inherent language-learning capabilities, which were referred to earlier in this paper, relate the acquisition of a second or subsequent language to the acquisition of a first language. As such they are concerned with acquisition of the skills in Column 1 of Table 1, and methodologies designed to encourage 'natural' language acquisition can only apply to such skills. The items listed in Column 2, being of a different quality, are taught even to native speakers, and thus, where need dictates their inclusion in an ESP syllabus, we would expect formal instruction as well as organized syllabuses to have a place.

9. Major Issues

The major issues for the syllabus designer in ESP concern the relationship between the language itself and the activities for which it is used. If, in order to use the language effectively in real situations, the learner must acquire enabling skills, as Munby (1978) claims, we need to learn much more about the nature of these various skills, and about the ways in which they can best be acquired. Work of this kind may help to resolve the question of where and in what degree a syllabus for non-native speakers can be similar to one designed for native speakers.

More investigation is needed into the relationship between the informally acquired language skills and the skills which are taught. If the former 'feed' the latter in any respect (that is, if primary language skills exist), there are serious implications for the course designer who chooses to ignore them. It is certain that these processes are very complex and that while some skills may safely be rejected, others will prove useful stages in learning a language for specific purposes as well as in improving communication among native speakers. Such issues need to be discussed in the light of pedagogic, linguistic and psycholinguistic understanding. The matter is one of some urgency since practice is overtaking us.

Notes

1. These four uses of the term 'skill' are merely descriptions. This is not an attempt at a discrete classification.
2. For a development of this report, see Hobsbaum, 'Standards of Written Expression among Undergraduates', in this volume.
3. I am grateful to Nikolas Coupland for reminding me of this point. See also his paper 'Aims and Attitudes in Teaching Communication Studies and English for Specific Purposes: the Challenge of Sociolinguistics', in this volume.

4. (See Table 1). Although 'reference skills' does appear in Munby's Taxonomy of Language Skills, this, in fact, is inconsistent with his stated views (page 6) since in his terminology 'use of dictionaries', for example, would appear to be an 'activity'.

References

BBC, *Zarabanda, A BBC Television Course for Beginners in Spanish*, London: BBC Publications, 1971.

BBC, *Digame, A Television and Radio Course for Beginners in Spanish*, London; BBC Publications, 1978.

BLUNDELL, J., HIGGENS, J. and MIDDLEMISS, N. *Function in English*, Oxford; Oxford University Press, 1982.

CORDER, S. P. *Introducing Applied Linguistics*. Harmondsworth: Penguin Education, 1973.

EDGE, J. and SAMUDA, V. 'Methodials: The Role and Design of Material and Method', in Richards, D. (ed.), *Communicative Course Design*, SEAMEO Regional English Language Centre, Singapore, 1981.

GREGORY, M. 'Aspects of varieties differentiation', *Journal of Linguistics*, 3, 2, 1967.

HERBOLICH, J. 'Box Kites' in Swales, J. *Episodes in ESP*, Oxford: Pergamon, 1984.

HOBSBAUM, P., KAY, C., MILNE, R. and HEWITT, R. H. *et al. Report to the Senate from Glasgow University Literacy Group*, 1981 (mimeo).

JOHNSON, K. 'The 'Deep End' Strategy in Communicative Language Teaching,' *MEXTESOL Journal*, 4, 2, 1980.

JOHNSON, K. 'Five Principles in a 'Communicative' Exercise Type', in *Communicative Syllabus Design and Methodology*, Oxford: Pergamon, 1982.

JONES, L. *Functions of English*, Cambridge: Cambridge University Press, 1977.

MUNBY, J. *Communicative Syllabus Design*, Cambridge: Cambridge University Press, 1978.

NATIONAL CONGRESS ON LANGUAGES IN EDUCATION, *Report of Working Party C.* London: CILT, January 1980.

NEWMARK, L. and REIBEL, D. A. 'Necessity and Sufficiency in Language Learning', *IRAL*, VI, 2, 1968.

RICHTERICH, R. and CHANCERELL, J. L. *Identifying the Needs of Adults Learning a Foreign Language*, Oxford: Pergamon, 1980.

ROBINSON, P. *ESP (English for Specific Purposes)*, Oxford: Pergamon, 1980.

TECHNICIAN EDUCATION COUNCIL SPECIALIST PANEL II (General and Communication Studies), *Bases for Curriculum Development in General and Communication Studies for Certificate, Diploma and Higher Award Programmes*, Technician Education Council, 1981.

WILLIAMS, R. C. 'The Potential Benefits to the ESP Profession from Greater Awareness of Developments and Practices in L1 Communication Skills Learning', in McDonough, J. and French, A. (eds.), *ELT Documents 112 — The ESP Teacher: Role, Development and Prospects*, The British Council, 1981.

Editor's Comment

Meriel Bloor raises an important issue in EFL syllabus design: namely, the inter-relationship between the target language and the communicative activities in which that language is to be used. At present (particularly in ESP) the pendulum has perhaps swung too far towards 'practice/exposure' to those activities, with insufficient prior investigation as to their desirable inherent characteristics. And it is precisely in this area that the experience of the L1 Communication Studies profession has such a lot to offer ESP. For example, research by Gage and his associates at Stanford (1972) has a great deal to tell ESP about the characteristics of "good oral explaining"; similarly, Kirkman's investigations (1980) into desirable professional scientific writing style should certainly have a place in ESP syllabus design.

Conversely, the rigorous Needs Analysis approaches to EFL syllabus design (exemplified by Munby) are now beginning to be felt in L1 Communication Studies, where 'rule-of-thumb' measures have held centre-stage for rather too long.

GAGE, N. L. in Westbury, I. and Bellack, A. (eds.), *Research into Classroom Processes*, New York, Teachers College Press, ch. 9. **10, 11, 16,** 1972.
KIRKMAN, J. *Good Style in Scientific and Engineering Writing*, London: Pitman, 1980.

RCW

TEACHING HIGHER INTELLECTUAL SKILLS: WHY ARE OUR COURSES NOT MORE SIMILAR?

John Cowan, Elspeth Bingham, Derek Fordyce and John McCarter

Heriot-Watt University

Introduction

Our department has a design course in which part of the time is devoted to developing the creative and analytical skills which a designer must exercise. The activities presently included in this programme are a consequence of a variety of influences and experiences — in design teaching (Cowan, 1981), educational research (Cowan, 1978) and process analysis (Cowan, 1980). But the final form is more important than the history of its evolution. For it has been transferred from a third year course in creative design to a first year course in communication skills — and, later, to elements of a new course in problem-solving. The success of these transfers confirms that those who teach for higher intellectual skills have more in common — and therefore more to interchange — than has hitherto been appreciated. It is that common ground which we attempt to explore in this paper.

1. Essential Characteristics of the Design Course

These are the features which emerged in our programme of activities to engender and develop skills in creative design:
1. The learning is experiential — since the aim of the learner is *not* to acquire knowledge, but to develop skills.
2. Each activity is made up from two or more similar items, arranged to present a more demanding challenge as the activity progresses.
3. The activities are combined in a programme which concentrates first on the more basic skills, and then on the higher level ones.
4. Within a given activity, any particular type of experience is quickly repeated, so that familiarization can be followed by learning and consolidation.
5. Reflection on process is encouraged, as a means of improving performance and ability.
6. The subject matter chosen for all activities must be directly relevant to the main course of study. Since the process is regarded as a means to an end, the product in every activity must be immediately relevant and obviously useful.

7. The teaching approach is 'inter-disciplinary', being concerned both with skills training and with the mastery of a particular aspect of engineering subject matter, or with the resolution of a real engineering problem.

2. The First Transfer

Circumstances within our department called for the creation of a course in technical communication skills, taught at first-year level. It seemed feasible to build on our experience with the third-year design teaching. We adopted that model, and developed from it a programme which consisted essentially of one 2-hour activity per fortnight, followed in the summer term by a major project which drew everything together.

A typical 2-hour activity required the student to
  — prepare beforehand
  — tackle a real and relevant communication task
  — criticise his own work, or that of his peers
  — reflect on the process, prior to an immediate repetition of it in more demanding circumstances
  — use and consolidate lower level skills when working on higher level ones.

It will be apparent that all the main features of the design course were retained, although the context was totally different, and the style of activity was rather more highly organized, in view of the inexperience of the students.

The communication skills course was deemed effective by both staff and students (Cowan *et al.*, 1982), and had an effect on the standard of communication in the department which was discernible by members of staff who did not teach on this course.

3. Another Transfer

A consequence of the favourable evaluations of the pilot-scheme tests of activities for the communication skills course was a further proposal, this time for a first year course in problem-solving. We are presently exploring this in pilot-scheme experiments, planned along the same lines as were followed in the other two programmes.

4. Discussion

We are conscious that we could equally well adopt other teaching methods, such as small groups which would respond to tasks in their own ways, without the provision of a firm programme and with an emphasis on task rather than on structure. Certainly we appreciate that we will need to change our methods in the second stage of any of these courses, when we try to take

the learning further. So we may be taking the easy way out by simply transferring a formula for the initial first stages of skills training — simply because
it has proved successful for us. Nevertheless we feel that it is useful and valid
to transfer elements which appear to be common to most intellectual skills
training.

The transfers have thus been conscious and deliberate for us. So we feel it
time to ask if there *is* the significant similarity which we claim between the
various types of higher intellectual skills which teachers seek to develop in
tertiary courses. For, if there *is* such common ground, it surely behoves us all
to look for a higher degree of transferability of ideas and of philosophy
between one such course and another than is the case at present.

5.   Common Ground

In terms of the forms of activity which we are presently using in our teaching,
we can see no real difference between design, communication and problem-
solving. We can take a useful format from one of these courses and transfer
it to another setting, changing little more than the subject matter, the task
wording and the questions asked in the documentation. Why should this be
so, if the fundamental skills are not the same or very similar?

As a tentative analysis, and to provoke conference discussion, we suggest
that all learners who aspire to higher intellectual skills
  — will learn effectively by doing and by reflecting on that activity
  — will learn most effectively if they build up the total ability, in their own
    ways, from a number of component skills
  — must always be given the opportunity to exercise the skills in a relevant
    context, otherwise the learning experiences will be shallow, meaning-
    less or misleading
  — will respond positively to constructive comments, suggestions and
    appraisal from peers.

These assertive suggestions imply that certain styles of activity are
appropriate in teaching programmes where intellectual skills are the main
priority. Out list of characteristics would not, for instance, apply to courses
where the students are *told* how to communicate or *taught* how to solve
problems. Our assertions imply that teachers should design an experiential
series of small group activities in which separate skills and total ability each
receive particular and separate attention. Peer-group appraisal should be
encouraged for formative assessments, even if summative assessment
remains the responsibility of the teacher. And the topic, whether
communication or problem-solving or design, should always be taught in the
midst of situations where the students are genuinely communicating, or
genuinely problem-solving or genuinely designing.

In Table 1 we explore further the similarity between the frameworks we have

	Creative Design (Third Year)	Communication Skills (First Year)	Problem-Solving Methods (First Year)
TASK	Development of analytical ability	The preparation and presentation of analyses of observed situations	Identification of first stages of personal algorithm of problem-solving in applied science
PRIORITY	Helping the students to see that an adequate design approach must be based on the principle of thorough and generally explicit analysis of the problem	Helping the students to develop the ability to present analytical descriptions in a logical manner, often identifying gaps or weaknesses in the information through the use of such a framework	Helping the students to develop a personal methodology which will enable them to tackle unseen problems where hitherto they 'wouldn't know where to start'
DIFFICULTY	Students want to 'skip over' this stage, and move immediately to synthesis	Presentations are normally rushed and illogical, showing no signs of having been properly assembled	Students are ashamed to 'waste' time on this stage, as they feel that only stupid learners need to do so
SOLUTION	Present a range of techniques and styles / Explore them / Use them in tasks specifically restricted to analysis	Generate a range of techniques and styles / Explore them / Use them in a further task which is specifically restricted to analysis	Identify the range of techniques and styles presently used / Explore them and compare them / Use some of them in tasks specifically restricted to the first analytical stages, and compare the experiences
FRAMEWORK	Do it / Review it / Do it again—on a different problem / Consolidate and extrapolate the experience to other examples of vital problems in this part of the subject	As design, but the repeated experience may be on the same problem	As design

Table 1. *Course Frameworks for First and Third-Year Activities*

used in our course activities. This analysis appears to endorse our view that a format which proved useful for developing one type of skill has been readily transferred into other contexts, without being significantly influenced by the natures of the skills concerned.

6. Detailed Comparison

Consider the design student in Column 1 of Table 1. He could be a non-rugby player, called on to design a better scrummaging machine than is presently offered on the open market. He may not even know what a scrummaging machine is! He certainly has no conception (at present) of improvements in the basic design which might be either desirable or possible. His (somewhat natural) tendency is to rush off to the catalogues or to the Scottish Rugby Union, to find out what is presently available so that he may imitate that and perhaps improve it by eliminating a few of the minor weaknesses. In contrast, the aim of his teacher at this stage in the overall learning situation is to help the student to appreciate that he will be a much more successful designer if he devotes a fair amount of time to analysing the nature of the problem and basing his subsequent design work on that analysis.

Rather different, at first sight, is the analytical challenge which confronts the first-year student in our problem-solving class example in Column 3. For this student is called on to integrate a variety of mathematical expressions — and he encounters difficulties in so doing. When the teacher demonstrates the answer — and shows, step-by-step, how it is obtained, the student under-stands each step and finds no difficulty with the solution. But when he is faced with the next mathematical expression to be integrated, he does not know what the first step should be on this occasion. His need is for a personal algorithm of problem-solving which will be effective for him; and the part of that algorithm on which attention must be focussed is the development of his ability to analyse such problems in his own terms, thereby unearthing or pointing to suggestions about the vital first steps in successful solutions.

Notice that, as far as the learners are concerned, the two situations would be perceived as quite different. The design student would be quite happy to rush on and 'botch' the analysis stage; he has an imperfect methodology which will enable him to obtain some sort of a solution; the teacher's problem, as far as this student is concerned, is to convince him of the *need* for analysis. In contrast, our frustrated mathematician is all too aware of the need for a methodology — because he can make no progress without it. *His* difficulty is that it must be a methodology which he can understand and utilize — and accept into his repertoire without feeling a second class citizen in con-sequence.

In both cases the fundamental need is concentration on the process of analysis. The common ground is evident, although teachers and learners, faced with the immediate teaching and learning priorities, would not see the parallel as obviously as our table makes apparent.

The surface dissimilarities are, we suggest, even more apparent in the case of the example taken from the communication skills course. In this case the immediate priority in the minds of both the students and the teacher is that of effective communication. The student may have gathered together the information about a case study which is to describe a badly cracked structure and discuss possible reasons for the damage. He now wishes to convey that description, and his interpretation of it, to the reader; and he is not quite sure how he should go about this task. He is tempted to resort to a feeble imitation of the essay style which he acquired at school when writing with totally different subject matter. Our experiences suggest that the faults in the final product are more likely to be a consequence of inability to analyse data and to present that analysis to others than of lack of mere communication skills. If we are correct in that belief, it implies that analysis is therefore once more the real focus of this activity.

We doubt if the teacher or the learner in this instance would see much common ground with the third-year class in the design studio. Yet students in all three classes seek to analyse data and convey their findings to others — with different emphases on the components of similar tasks. And so we emphasize once again that the apparent obvious parallel may well be worthy of exploration, for just that reason.

Our table emphasizes that teachers have really the same underlying aim in each of the activities described; they are focussing the attention of the student on one facet or another of the process of analysis. Similarly we believe that most courses which seek to develop higher intellectual skills will be dealing, at one time or another, with processes associated with the same intellectual skills (although not only with analysis, of course). It is only because these skills are applied in totally different contexts that they need be presented to the students in situations which will seem quite different to them.

Summary

We admit frankly that this paper is in a different form from that which we envisaged when we began the first draft. At that time we wished to convey something of our experience in transferring styles of teaching and learning activity from one type of situation to another. We felt that higher intellectual skills might have something in common, from the teacher's point of view; and we wished to argue that this common ground should be explored and exploited.

As we have tried to present our argument, it has become more and more apparent to us that teachers of higher intellectual skills are concerned with the same skills, in different contexts; the only difference between us lies in the ways in which particular situations require these skills to be expressed.

Returning to the title of the paper, we conclude that those who teach higher intellectual skills *should* make greater use of the experiences and innovations of others who share similar goals—and would then produce course styles which probe the common fundamental issues with more rigour and purpose.

References

COWAN, J. 'Design education based on an expressed statement of the design process', *Proceedings of the Institution of Civil Engineering*, Part 1, **70,** November 1981.

COWAN, J. 'Freedom in Selection of Course Content: A Case Study of A Course without a Syllabus', *Studies in Higher Education* 3 (2), October 1978.

COWAN, J. 'Improving the recorded protocol', *Programmed Learning and Educational Technology,* **17** (3), August 1980.

COWAN, J. BINGHAM, E. G., FORDYCE, D. S. E. and McCARTER, J. 'Seeking (and using) a tentative hierarchy of communication skills', Paper presented to Sheffield Conference on Communication Skills, Sheffield Polytechnic, April 1982.

Editor's Comment

Many (most?) students of engineering and science are reluctant to accept that a course in 'English' has anything to do with them. This paper from Heriot-Watt emphasises that poor communication in science and technology is usually a result not of faulty grammar but of inadequate understanding of the communication task. Students respond better if they are invited to analyse a problem and suggest a solution. Thus, CS programmes should involve analysis of communication processes and problems, not just 'tinkering with the English'.

John Cowan and his colleagues stress the need always to exercise skills in a relevant context. They also stress the value of appraisal from peers. It is perhaps difficult to arrange this efficiently in L2 classes; but group discussion, with all members of the group invited to join in finding the most effective way of tackling a communication task, helps greatly to dispel the view that the writer alone has difficulties in communicating. It is helpful to remove the focus from each individual's efforts, and place it on the intrinsic difficulties (and intriguing challenges) in common communication tasks.

JK

COMMUNICATIONS: THE INTERFACE BETWEEN EDUCATION AND INDUSTRY

MARY KING

University of Bradford

1. The Background to Some Problems at the Education/Industry Interface

In a discussion document presented to the Headmasters' Conference in 1981, David Emms, Head of Dulwich College, described the over-specialization of the school curriculum in England and Wales as lying 'at the base of our industrial difficulties as far as inadequate management is concerned'. He pointed out that the three A-level system has failed to produce (i) the young people of all-round ability so urgently needed by industry; (ii) science students who can express themselves cogently on paper or orally; (iii) arts students who have sufficient awareness of scientific functions and (iv) young people who at 18 have a sufficiently wide range of choice before them. The current emphasis on the need for a more integrated, systemic approach to the curriculum is part of a growing realization that the traditional pre-emptive nature of sixth-form and university education is revealing a near-disastrous inability to attract creative and innovative young people into the world of production and technology, and to educate them to master and direct, or even to cope with, sociotechnological change. There is an acute awareness amongst industrialists that the initiative in this area is eluding Britain and passing to Japan and the continent. The historical pattern is being repeated today in which during the nineteenth century the intelligentsia took fright and retreated from a world of technology which they did not understand into 'the world of the privileged mind' (Nuttgens, 1982). However, in a world in which we can no longer take refuge from economic reality in easy colonial markets, or rely upon the Indian National Debt to make good or conceal the deficits in the productive sector of our economy, we cannot escape, either, from the hard fact that 'successful manufacturing industry is everywhere the basis of national prosperity and economic dynamism . . . Manufacturing is the key to *growth*' (Eatwell, 1982).

Our traditional practice puts emphasis on early specialization into 'arts' or 'sciences' at school and the concomitant commitment at university level to the 'pursuit of problems . . . largely of disciplinary interest'. To meet this sensed inappropriateness, some educators talk of a return at sixth form level to something like the old five-subject School Certificate (Blume, 1981). Universities and polytechnics are beginning to proliferate a range and variety of multidisciplinary courses, in which 'communication', in various forms and guises, often features as an input. The problem with many of the projected solutions is that instead of examining critically the demands which will be made upon students by technological change in their future careers and analysing the implications for society in general and education in particular, they tend to look philosophically and methodologically to the past. Invoking an imaginary golden age of general education, many courses substitute an aggregate of old forms of specialisms for the discredited overspecialization. Industry, for its part, often fails to offer any very precise guidance about its needs or requirements, is slow to define and accept responsibility for its own educative role, and tends to restrict itself to calls for a return to the three R's in our schools, while lamenting the lack of innovative talent in its graduate recruits.

At degree level, joint honours courses of the $A + B + n$ type have evolved, where A and B all too often are random combinations of hitherto single disciplines. Not enough consideration has been given to whether the subjects or options offered are being taught so as to create the educational interaction and mutual support which are essential if we are "to combat technological illiteracy among the arts and humanities students, and . . . social and humanitarian illiteracy among the technocrats" (Stonier, 1977). When there is insufficient conceptual or methodological integration, students can be worse off than before. As staff battle to make of their particular module or input a miniature honours degree, overburdened and confused students are condemned for their inability to measure up to the standards of 'the good old days'.

One solution to this problem may be to call in 'the communications specialist' to aid the ailing patients by implementing a remedial course of action. The expectation of colleagues may well be that regular not too time-consuming doses of various skills from the communications pharmacopoeia will cure the ills of 'illiteracy' and bring about the desired integration of knowledge and skills. When this fails to happen, it leads initially to disappointment on both sides. This, in turn, gives rise to much recrimination, during which we hear at monotonously regular intervals that scientists, technologists and engineers cannot express themselves cogently or communicate to anyone outside their own hyperspecialist areas. And we are informed, not without some justification, that arts people, including some lecturers in communications, are technologically illiterate and/or ignorant of 'the real world of industry'. Between the Scylla of eclecticism and the Charybdis of remedial teaching, the ship of communications all too often founders before it is properly launched, and certainly before it has time to chart its course through unknown waters.

2. The Challenge to Curriculum Planning

It is scarcely an exaggeration to claim that these difficulties cannot be resolved by a simple, or simplistic, addition of communications to any course which aims at educating rather than merely training students for creative professional careers in industry. Students today must be enabled to respond flexibly, and to take initiatives, in situations where holistic thinking and the ability to anticipate problems and synthesize solutions are at least of equal importance as factual information or analytical skills. In industry, each problem is unique, and as technologies became more complex and interact more profoundly than ever with society, it is vital for the successful initiation and direction of change to be able to operate in terms of dynamic, interactive sociotechnological systems. In such a context the challenge to manufacturing technologists is great since they will require experience in manufacturing techniques, mechanical and control system operation, programming and application of computers to manufacturing processes, and the operation of complex manufacturing systems. In addition, the ability to work with people is an essential element because of the need to liaise between management, specialist service groups and production operatives (Charnley, 1977).

Any communications contribution which fails to relate closely to these complex needs inevitably invites all the problems from which general studies, for example, notoriously suffers. This is true whether the input is orientated towards developing writing programmes, oral competence, reading, comprehension, and library skills, etc., or concentrates on teaching the theory and practice of organizational communications. For the teacher of communications, the costs of battling against student apathy and the charge of irrelevance can be enormous.

The often ambivalent attitude towards communications in the academic context contrasts sharply with the importance accorded by industry and the professions to the ability to communicate, and to understand the role of communications in organizational structures. Repeated surveys have called attention to the high value attributed to this ability, while "successful engineers in industry typically cite lack of communications training as the most significant defect in their own professional preparation" (Baker, 1982). Often enough, it must be said, the precise nature of the desired skills is not very clearly defined: much research of a collaborative nature between industry and education needs to be carried out in this field.

3. A New Approach to Curriculum Development: Industrial Technology and Management

Awareness of the need to change this state of affairs led to the design, starting some twelve years ago, of the honours degree sandwich course in Industrial Technology and Management (IT&M) at the University of Bradford. The course was developed to meet the challenge to education of technological change: in particular, the need to develop intellectual flexibility, professional adaptability and innovative skills. Industrial innovation requires many qualities, amongst which may be identified:

★ the ability to relate theory to practice *in new ways*

★ flexibility in relation to people, organizations and technology
★ creative thinking, including divergent and synthetic strategies
★ awareness of and sensitivity to organizational behaviour
★ sensitivity to the interactions between technology and society
★ the ability to communicate and work in interdisciplinary teams
★ a sound grasp of science (including social sciences) and technology, since "when an innovator anticipates, he is doing no more than choosing the new front where the technical action will be" (Olmer, 1982).

In response to these needs, the implications for education include:

★ the need to integrate academic inputs with students' industrial experience
★ abandonment of the rigid single-discipline approach, which all too often pre-empts flexibility
★ an emphasis on symbolic thinking, self-motivation, and open-ended and project-based learning
★ development of theoretical and practical knowledge of organizational structures and behaviour patterns
★ deliberate fostering of communications skills, including personal and group presentation skills and techniques
★ concentration on developing an interdisciplinary approach to the formulation, definition and solution of problems
★ integration of the natural, the social and the engineering sciences into a new *science of industrial activity*

Because of its centrality to technological development and social change, *the nature of the production process itself* was selected as the integrating focus of the new course. This focus on production had two immediate, and vitally important consequences, not least for the teaching of communications: (i) it drew attention to the need to build a course *not* from an aggregate of single-subject modules; and (ii) it required members of the teaching team to work out new ways of selecting from, organizing, and communicating to each other as well as to students, relevant inputs from their own subjects. The common point of reference acts as a powerful check upon the chief danger of multidisciplinarity—the danger of fragmentation. The new conceptual and pedagogical requirements meant that communications itself was quickly perceived as having a crucial role to play in the exploration and elucidation of the inter-relationships between areas of the curriculum. Evidence of the School's commitment to the principles and practice of integration is its unorthodox but highly successful policy, since its inception, of admitting A-level students from both science and arts backgrounds, and its appointment of a communications lecturer on a full-time basis to the multidisciplinary staff team. Neither of these policies, it must be said, has been implemented without opposition from 'conventional' academic circles. Both, however, are now recognized, however grudgingly at times, to have anticipated much recent thinking about new approaches to education for industry.

4. The Role of Communications as an Integrating Discipline

The focus of the course in IT&M is the study of the nature of production as a sociotechnological process: "the strength and success of the course is in studying interactions between areas of hitherto single disciplines arising from the nature of industrial activity" (Page, 1982). The ability to use language and to think symbolically is fundamental to creative and productive activity, going hand-in-hand with tool-using in the centrality of its contribution to human evolution. Communications, like production, is also essentially transdisciplinary. As a result, the communications lecturer is in an especially favourable position to be able to establish for students the conceptual framework and learning strategies necessary for a new synthesis of theory and practice. If students are to begin to appreciate the need for such a synthesis, they require a basic unifying model to which they can continually refer. The introduction and exploration of such a provisional working model is one of the major objectives of the initial communications input. Complementary practical activities include the fostering of new kinds of study skills, both cooperative and self-motivating, and of team-work activities. Most teaching and learning on the course take place in seminar teams comprising combinations of students with arts and sciences backgrounds.

The basic model of industry which is offered to the students, together with an introduction to systems thinking, is that of production as a dynamic, open, interactive and constantly changing system in which we have

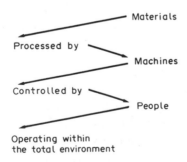

Processed by → Materials

Machines

Controlled by →

People

Operating within
the total environment

Looked at in terms of the input required in order to arrive at a scientific understanding of the system, the model begins to explain why the course structure covers five inter-related areas rather than subjects:

       MATERIALS TECHNOLOGY
       ENGINEERING OR MACHINE TECHNOLOGY
       PEOPLE IN INDUSTRY
       THE SOCIAL CONTEXT OF PRODUCTION
  and the   QUANTATIVE TECHNIQUES

which are indispensable for the planning and control of almost every process and function in industry today.

Communications is located within the area of the social context of production, and also operates on a workshop basis as a link between all of the other components, including the projects and industrial placements. Staff emphasize, and students rapidly learn, that communications is part of the social context of production in a very intrinsic way: production and society are interdependent phenomena which rely upon language for their very existence. A basic systemic model of production, which also has a diachronic dimension, enables students to approach the science of industrial activity as the study of a complex system located within the historically changing system of the total environment. It also prepares the ground for their study, before their first industrial placements at the end of the first year, of formal communications and organization (C&O) theories and models. In turn, this study of organizations as systems provides a frame of reference to which they can begin to refer their practical experiences in industry. Familiarity with systems-thinking offers an extremely useful basis for the critical analysis of C&O theory. Systems-modelling also provides an integrating induction for arts and sciences students into the inter-related contributions of the various 'single' disciplines to an understanding of production.

During their study of the social context of production, as in most other areas of the course, students regularly prepare and present seminar papers. In the social context work in Year One, they are asked to present systems-orientated accounts of phenomena or processes which are conceptually subsumed into one of four main subsystems, identified on an evolutionary/diachronic basis as inorganic, organic, biological and human systems. These presentations are also used to develop information retrieval and synthesis skills, study skills, team work, written and graphical communications, and oral presentation skills. Thus the academic work provides the basis for practice of the kinds of communicative skills which are invaluable in industry.

Complementing this input is an extended and assessed communications exercise. Students are required in Term One to write a formal report on a material which is used or produced in industry. Again, the approach is broadly systemic, and both individual work and team work are required. In Term Two, all attend a series of communications workshops on the techniques of making oral presentations and using visual aids. Each, as a member of a five-person team, makes a 15 minute videotaped oral presentation based on the report topic. The importance placed on this exercise is underlined by the presence of the Professor of Industrial Technology as part of the audience and as a co-assessor. In Term Three, students are prepared, with a series of formal C&O inputs and simulation exercises, for their first industrial experience. The simulated interviews are coordinated with 'the real thing', as they are also interviewed by firms during this term for their placements in industry.

5. The Education-Industry Interface

It is only when students are actually involved in working in industry that much of what they learn begins to be perceived in terms of its relevance as well as its limitations. To ensure that they critically relate theory to practice, they are required to write a report, for both firm and university, on their progress in industry: a challenging exercise in audience orientation. When they return to university, they also write up a further report, on C&O in industry. They must now distinguish between models and realities and try to account for correlations and discrepancies. During this writing-up period, the communications input concentrates on a more intensive and critical series of discussions and analyses of the role of communications in industry, than is possible in Year One. At this stage it has become possible to draw upon the wide variety of student experience in a really meaningful context.

Once again in Term Two, students are required to make a video-presentation, this time based upon their written reports on C&O. They have the opportunity therefore, to reflect objectively upon, and debrief each other about, C&O in industrial practice, *relating this debriefing to C&O theories and models*. As the year progresses, demands upon their skills as communicators are increased by project work and the prospect of vivas as well as by the imminence of a second period in industry. They are now ready to respond with a lively sense of relevance and, indeed, urgency, to case-studies and simulation exercises. They also know they may have to cope with industry's too frequent *underestimation* of what they can contribute, and they know that information in industry can be part of a power game which differs from the academic context.

This returns us to the question of the importance of encouraging industry itself to identify and assume responsibility for its own educative role. In our society, the interests of education and industry are not, and indeed cannot be, identical; but they do need to be much more carefully considered in relation to each other. The advantages for the educator are that by working at the interface between industry and education, one remains acutely aware of the nature and social implications of technological change—as well as of the results of failure to change in the right direction.

In his opening address at the recent SEFI conference at Delft, on 'The education of the engineer for innovative activity', Professor Olmer asked the question "Will the future of our enterprises, of our industrial societies and indeed the future of our geopolitical world . . . be a purely *cybernetic* one where the rules create themselves as the structures give way under the pressures put upon them, or will there be *other possible futures* that could come to pass through humanity's capacity for imagination and innovation?" (Olmer, 1982). The communications lecturer has a special responsibility and privilege (sanctioned historically by the role of language in human creativity, and in the very process of humanization itself) to ensure that we educate people who are able not merely to choose, but also to realize those possible futures which *will* use science and technology to benefit, not to destroy, humankind.

References

BAKER, R. 'Developing teaching strategies for the improvement of language/thinking skills appropriate to science/engineering students', in *Proceedings of Eighth International Conference on Improving University Teaching*, Berlin 1982, **III**, p. 671.
BLUME, E. British Association for the Advancement of Science Lecture, September, 1981. Reported in *Times Higher Education Supplement*, 4.9.81.
CHARNLEY, J. 'What's wrong with making it?', *New Scientist*, 31.3.77, p. 767.
EATWELL, J. *Whatever Happened to Britain?*, London, 1982, p.51.
EMMS, D. *HMC Schools and British Industry*, Winchester, 1981 (mimeo).
NUTTGENS, P. 'Living with technology', (Second Napier memorial Lecture), June 1982, *Times Higher Education Supplement*, 11.6.82, pp. 3/4.
OLMER, P. 'Demotivating factors in higher education, or how to snuff out the innovatory instinct in our students', SEFI address to Delft conference, June 1982, p. 18. (mimeo).
PAGE, C. W. 'Some notes on possible future trends in Industrial Technology', paper presented to the School of Industrial Technology and Management, Bradford University, June 1982, (mimeo).
STONIER, T. 'A profile of the post-industrial society', in *Strategies for Change in a Technological Society*, Conference Report, University of Bath Science and Technology Education Centre, December 1977, p. 7 (mimeo).

Editor's Comment

Mary King urges us to abandon outmoded views of what constitutes a proper pattern of education, and to base our teaching on analysis of the demands that will be made upon students in their future careers.

She is firmly in accord with John Cowan and his colleagues in insisting that we must encourage an analytical approach to problems, and must teach flexibility of response.

Practising CS teachers will have found, with King, among many of their engineering and science colleagues a hope, that "regular not too time-consuming doses of various skills from the communications pharmacopoeia will cure the ills of 'illiteracy' and bring about the desired integration of knowledge and skills". Attempts to help students to develop communication skills often founder because special-subject teachers support courses or other programmes *only provided* that those courses do not disturb the students' concentration on their 'real' work. 'Add-on' CS teaching is never likely to be as effective as genuinely integrated teaching. For that reason, King's experience at Bradford is a valuable resource for us all, and has many threads in common with the accounts of collaborative teaching—Dudley-Evans, Gee *et al.* and de Escorcia—reported in this volume.

JMS

III. Approaches to the Teaching of Writing

IMPROVING STUDENT WRITING: AN INTEGRATED
APPROACH TO CULTURAL ADJUSTMENT

Brigid Ballard

The Australian National University, Canberra, Australia

Introduction

On entering university, a student is starting on a process of socialization into a new cultural system. If that socialization is to be effective, the student must acquire the language, the interests and the behaviours appropriate to the new culture. This process is particularly complex as the university cultural system consists of many distinctive sub-cultures, each based in a different discipline and embodied in a separate department. Each discipline has its distinctive content, orientation, language and methodology which must be recognized and learned. The first-year student, who is probably enrolled in courses in four different departments, must therefore master four separate sub-cultures as soon as possible. He is inducted into these disciplines—at the formal level—through lectures, tutorials, laboratory work and reading, but it is through *written* assignments that the success of his acculturation is most commonly judged. The acquisition of cultural literacy, therefore, becomes both the key to and the measure of academic progress.

1. The Problems of Cultural Adjustment

In a pamphlet written for academic staff at The Australian National University (ANU), staff in the Study Skills Unit have identified some common areas of difficulty for first-year students. New students characteristically have problems in:
- distinguishing between disciplines, i.e. recognizing that each discipline has its own distinctive methods of analysis
- learning to use competently the highly specialized varieties of language which derive from these distinctive methods of analysis
- coping with differences between secondary and tertiary level study within the same discipline
- coping with, or even comprehending, the variety of departmental expectations they must meet

  — learning to think critically and analytically
  — recognizing and making distinctions between details and underlying concepts
  — evaluating the quality of their own and others' work; ceasing to equate quantity with quality, and effort with achievement.

These problems stem from a disjunction between the style of learning which the student has successfully practised at school and that now required at university. We can illustrate this by looking at an example of the third problem specified above. A student at school faced with the essay topic 'What were the causes of the French revolution?' generally proceeds as though the question were susceptible of a certain answer. The task for him is essentially one of finding and summarizing the relevant information. For this he will go to his textbook, and perhaps one or two other sources when his notes seem incomplete. The university student, set exactly the same topic, must approach the task with a radically different understanding — and a different set of strategies. If he is in any way experienced, he will know that there is no single correct answer or interpretation; rather there are likely to be as many different interpretations as there are historians who have written on the subject. His task, therefore, is to read widely and critically; to identify differences in interpretation and the uses to which evidence has been put in the framing of these interpretations; and finally, however tentatively, to form and argue a judgement of his own. Learning has now become a much more complex and relativistic business despite the outward similarity of the tasks.

In coming to understand that questions no longer imply answers — or that for any one question there may be many acceptable answers — the student is learning one of the *general* rules of the university culture. Just as importantly, he must learn to recognize and apply the specific rules which obtain in different disciplinary contexts. In the case of history, he must understand the rules that determine what constitutes evidence, how sources may be treated, when personal expression is stylistically appropriate, etc. He must learn that the Victorian novel that has been set as a text for English, history and sociology courses will be treated in markedly different ways in each course.

2. Bridging the Gap

This view of the transition from school to university as a shift between cultures shapes the way we see our role as academic advisers to students at ANU. We are not so much teachers, counsellors or tutors as *interpreters*. We interpret the general intellectual culture of the university and we make students aware of the distinctions between the disciplinary sub-cultures. This attitude to our work has a number of important implications. It determines, for example, the materials we use. As far as possible, we use only materials brought to us by the students from their academic courses. We never attempt to teach 'study skills' in isolation from the actual context of the discipline being studied: if a law student seeks advice on revising for exams, we look at his own law lecture notes, course outlines, past exam papers, and draw on the experience of law students who passed the same course in the previous year. In the same way we do not teach 'essay writing' out of the context of the actual assignments students have been set in their courses; we are less inclined to teach 'skills' than to help a particular student work on a particular essay at a particular stage in his academic career.

2.1   Assisting the Individual Student

We work in the following way. The Communication and Study Skills Unit is part of Student Services, and its staff may be consulted by any of the 5000 undergraduates and 1000 postgraduates in the University. We have three professional staff, a secretary, and a photo-copier. Two of the advisers work in the area of language and study skills, and one is a specialist in maths and statistics. Most of our time, maybe 70%, is spent working with individuals; but we also run short courses and work in various ways with academic staff. A brief sketch of a typical morning of the Unit may be useful. The first student brings a preliminary draft of a botany essay on the taxonomy of plants ("It seems to be disorganized, somehow, and it's much too long but I don't see how I can condense it"); then comes a postgraduate overseas student who wants comment on the opening chapter of his PhD thesis on forestry, before he takes it to his supervisor, because he is having difficulty in formulating his hypothesis in acceptable English; then a shy first-year student who has just received back an essay in history with the comment that her style is weak ("I've always had poor expression, even at school"); then two economics students worried about how to prepare for their mid-year exam. Lunch is spent with a group of academic staff all teaching first-year students; over sandwiches we discuss the problems we know students are having with the next essay assignment ("Could it be a problem of wording? Maybe if it were reworded this way . . .?").

Each student's problem is different, and the strategies we adopt must vary appropriately. Thus the forestry student may need to look at a couple of theses in forestry to get a feel for an effective presentation of a hypothesis, and he may also need some specifically linguistic editing and some suggestions on how to raise the level of his expression. We may spend half an hour or more rewriting a couple of important paragraphs until they achieve the clarity he needs.

The first-year history student with 'poor expression', on the other hand, may present a more long-term and complex problem. The first step is to establish whether her problem is in fact a weakness in written expression (and if so, at which level: sentence structure? paragraphing? spelling? style?) or whether her disordered prose is merely symptomatic of a more fundamental failure in conceptual grasp. If it seems to be a weakness in written expression, we might begin by asking the student to read aloud part of her essay to see if she can pick up by ear the awkwardnesses and irregularities, and then proceed to discuss more specific points of grammatical structure. If her problem is control of her material, then we start at a more fundamental level: analysing the overall structure of her argument, looking at her use and development of paragraph units and, in the light of this, perhaps rewriting the opening paragraph together. In either case we would certainly go over the lecturer's comments and corrections with her — acting again as interpreters. Then we might look at a credit or distinction level essay on a related topic written by a student in the course the previous year (we collect such essays diligently from our students and find them an invaluable teaching resource) — not focussing so much on content as on the way in which the material has been organized and presented. And so it goes on.

In each case we are assisting the student to understand the adjustments that must be made in his thinking, his study habits and his writing, to meet the expectations of the course lecturer and the demands of the discipline. In each case also we treat the particular problem which brings the students to us as a point of entry to the integrated process of producing an essay; reading, analysing, planning, organizing, writing and editing are all inter-related and cannot effectively be worked on in isolation from each other or from the context, content and purpose of the actual course assignment.

2.2   The Place for Course Work

Although the major part of our time is spent with individual students, we also run short courses for small groups at various points in the academic year when demand for our services outstrips our resources. We run an 'Introduction to University Study' course before the start of the academic year; we occasionally run exam preparation groups; and we run at least two essay-writing courses — one just before the first essays are due in the first term, and another just after the first essays have been returned — times when students are highly motivated to seek help with their writing. In these writing courses (which meet twice a week for an hour each over a period of three weeks) students are sorted into groups of not more than ten on the basis of one academic course in common: in one group all students may be enrolled in anthropology, in another they may all be studying psychology. In this way, when we are discussing the problems in analysing essay topics, approaches to reading and research, and styles of analysis and writing, we can always use examples from the common course and then draw on comparisons from other units for which some students may also be writing essays.

We start at whatever point the students have reached: if it is early in the first term, we will begin by analysing the essay topics on which they are about to work; if the course is later in the year, we will be discussing the last essay everyone has received back. In all courses we usually cover the whole process of writing an essay, and the way in which we handle each aspect and the emphasis we give will depend on the stage the students are at and the problem areas they themselves specify. In general we cover the following aspects: analysing essay topics; efficient reading strategies; making selections from a reading list; note-taking; planning the structure of the argument; writing the first and successive drafts—emphasizing the differences in purpose and function between different drafts of the same material; editing; and, finally, ways of getting useful feedback from lecturers and other students.

Most of the materials for each course are provided by the students—their own essays, drafts and outlines, their course handouts and assigned readings, their own lecture notes. We do also provide some materials for common use:

1. A chapter from a book on Australian history, which we use for introducing students to skim-reading. This is supplemented by a handout analysing the structure of one paragraph, so we can move from the strategy of skimming by first sentences of paragraphs to some understanding of the function of the paragraph in academic writing as an idea unit. Students then follow this up by practising skimming when reading for their own courses, and by analysing the paragraph structure in their own essay writing.

2. A five-page handout which attempts to answer the common question: 'What do *they* want in an essay?' In order to discover the criteria for assessment which lecturers actually use (as distinct from the criteria they say they use, or the public platitudes about writing they offer in lectures or course handouts), we collected over 500 essays from many disciplines at all levels and typed out the final comments made by the lecturers. Then, disregarding the statements about content, we reviewed all the comments, both critical and positive, and found that, almost without exception, they fell into one of four categories. These then appear to be the essential criteria for an effective essay:
   It is expected that an essay:
   (1) will be clearly focussed on the set topic and will deal fully with its central concerns;
   (2) will be the result of wide and critical reading;
   (3) will present a reasoned argument; and
   (4) will be competently presented.
   Under each criterion we listed a selection of lecturers' comments, taken from the student essays, which fill out the meaning or implications of that criterion. This handout gives students some feel for what is expected of them in an academic essay, and it also prepares new students for the style of critical comments they may soon encounter.

3. A selection of two or three essays by past students which provide particularly clear examples of poor organization, or effective argument, or forceful introductions and conclusions.

4. A wide selection of first-year essays in all courses, donated by students who have taken our courses in previous years. We encourage students to browse through these to gain some idea of standards of marking and the level of writing required of them.

In these writing courses, students also bring their current essay drafts for discussion and we may spend one session in which they rewrite sections of their essay in the light of each other's comments. Underlying the whole course is the concept of essay writing as an extended process which integrates many skills and which can only be usefully taught in very close relation to the actual coursework in which each student is currently engaged.

2.3 Working with Departments

The remainder of our time is spent working with academic staff in a variety of ways to improve student writing, and to ameliorate the whole process of teaching and learning. This work takes many forms, depending on the manner in which the request for assistance originally comes to us, and so it may best be illustrated by a brief case study. One request came to the Unit from the Zoology Department: "Our first-year students' exam papers are illiterate; can the Unit do anything to improve their writing?" After discussion with the teaching staff, we discovered that, until the actual exam, students were not required to do any formal writing at all in the course and so had no practice in producing extended scientific prose. We arranged with the staff that the following year, in consultation with the Unit, they would set a short essay early in the first term. We were then slotted into their course schedule to give a lecture on writing scientific essays, drawing on the topic the students had been set. After the essays were handed in, they were graded and commented upon by the zoology staff according to criteria which had been worked out in discussion between lecturers, tutors and the Unit advisers. We then read all the essays and selected three or four examples of introductory paragraphs of varying effectiveness (but not the very best or the obviously unacceptable), and the same for middle paragraphs and conclusions. We duplicated these materials and then jointly led a tutorial session with each zoology tutor in which we got the students to discuss why they thought a particular paragraph was effective or weak. We focussed on rhetorical procedures and strategies, and the tutor provided the necessary disciplinary input. Through these discussions the students began to develop their own capacities for judging effective scientific prose, and the tutors became more aware of the stages through which a new student must go on the way to becoming a competent zoologist.

3. Second Language Speakers: the Double Cultural Shift

So far I have been describing the work we do with all undergraduates who come to our Unit: 90% of these would be Australian students, i.e. native speakers of (Australian) English. The remaining 10% — the overseas students and the second language speakers — have the same problems as Australian students compounded by additional difficulties with English and by the need to make a major cultural shift in their styles of thinking and learning. The majority of these students come to us identifying their problems as "I have trouble with English, especially writing it". They are also referred to the Unit by academic staff with the stereotypical comment, "This overseas student has turned in a very poor piece of work. He probably has trouble with his English. Can you people do something to fix him up?" Yet with these students we also find it more useful to work first on making sure they have begun the transition to the academic culture of the university. We discuss with them their approach to their work, their perceptions of the purposes of their courses and of the expectations of their lecturers and supervisors, their understanding of the demands of their assigned topic or the particular section of their thesis, and the style of argumentation and analysis that is required in their writing within the discipline in which they are studying. Then, and then only, do we turn to consideration of sentence structure and grammatical errors.

Many of these students have to make a twofold cultural adjustment in their approach to knowledge and to styles of learning. Not only must they make the same shifts to a university culture as Australian students must make, they must also make a major switch from the intellectual behaviour in which they have been trained in their own cultures, to the intellectual traditions which dominate Australian university studies. The following Table 1 sets out a simplified analysis of the socialization of students into various learning behaviours.

Teacher's attitude to knowledge	Student's learning approach	Student's learning strategies
conserving	reproductive	*Type of strategy*: Memorization and imitation *Activities*: Recognition and application of formulae *Characteristic question*: 'What?' *Aim*: 'Correctness'
extending	analytical	*Type of strategy*: Critical thinking *Activities*: Selection and recombination *Characteristic questions*: 'Why?' and 'How?' *Aim*: 'Simple' originality (reshaping material into a different pattern)
	speculative	*Type of strategy*: Deliberate search for new possibilities and explanations *Activity*: Hypothesizing *Characteristic question*: 'What if?' *Aim*: 'Creative' originality (totally new approach)

Table 1. *Styles of Learning*

If we apply this model to the Australian system of education, the conserving-reproductive approach to learning will largely characterize the high school level. Progress through university studies requires the student to shift to more analytical/speculative approaches, which presuppose the attitude that knowledge can be extended beyond the boundaries of what is currently known or accepted as true. Asian students, who form the great majority of overseas students studying in Australia, come from a system of education in which the traditional attitude to knowledge was that of conserving and preserving the wisdom of the past and of the elders. The modern school system in Asian countries, for a variety of reasons, continues this tradition with emphasis on respect for the authority of the teacher, on rote learning, and on passive classroom behaviour. For students raised in such a tradition, the shift to an analytical and critical approach to study is a major break with everything they have experienced in their previous education. Consequently, in our work as academic advisers, the problem of cultural interpretation becomes more complex, and more important, when assisting these students.

Again, let us look at some examples. A Japanese undergraduate, who had completed two years of economics successfully in Tokyo before coming to Australia, failed all his first-year economics courses at ANU and was sent to the Unit for 'help with his English' when repeating his first year studies in another Faculty. His command of English was extremely weak and his behaviour was firmly bound in Japanese traditions: he would bow whenever he spoke and would never turn his back when leaving the room. He brought the first draft of a history essay for us to work on. It was a straightforward comparison topic: 'Compare the ideas of X with the ideas of Y about education policy in the Meiji area'. The essay, which was written in poorly constructed English, began with an account of the life, upbringing and education of X up to the point at which he published his ideas about education policy. These ideas were briefly summarized. Then followed an exactly parallel treatment of Y. And there the essay finished. Obviously such an essay would be failed by the lecturer: "Irrelevant", "No analysis", "Where is your comparison of the two points of view?", "What is your conclusion about the relative merits of each?" — the critical comments would have covered every margin. The student, however, was quite clear why he had organized his thinking in this way. It was his purpose to display the necessary information which would enable the reader to understand how two eminent scholars could reach differing points of view without one being inferior to the other; his aim was to achieve harmony. And the essay finished where it did because, the student pointed out, it would be quite improper for a writer to tell his reader what to think, especially if the writer were a student and the reader his teacher. It is the duty of a writer, he explained, to present the relevant information so that the reader may reach his own conclusion uninfluenced by the views of the author.

Here we have a total dislocation in both expectation of and response to an essay topic, caused by a cultural difference in attitudes to the role of the student writer. Once it was explained to this student that he was expected to analyse the ideas of X, then analyse and compare the ideas of Y, and finally reach some evaluation of the strengths and weaknesses of each approach, then he could, with some initial misgivings, begin to do this. Throughout the year this student came regularly to the Unit with his essay drafts and we worked steadily on the structure of his argument, not on his grammar (which remained less than fluent). When he passed this course with a credit at the end of the year, his lecturer expressed this opinion of his work: "Ah, he has some problems with his English still, but you can see the fellow is really able to think well and that's what counts." In other words, this Japanese student was now thinking in a style which was recognizable as 'thinking' by the cultural standards of the Australian academic. Previously he had been 'thinking' in accordance with Japanese culture and the lecturer responded by seizing on the most obvious manifestation of his cultural failure—'weak English'.

Another aspect of this problem of conflicting cultural attitudes is exemplified in a doctoral thesis written in a style many of us will recognize (with sinking feelings). A Thai demography student had spent much time and labour on producing the first three chapters of his thesis on the fertility patterns of Chiangmai, a city in northern Thailand. He submitted these to his supervisor, and his manuscript was returned with a line through the first two chapters and the terse comment "Irrelevant. Start straight in by introducing your data on fertility patterns"—and the student's two months work was down the drain. A reading of his chapters made the source of his difficulty obvious. His first chapter covered the geography, climate, history, Monarchy and culture of Thailand. The second chapter covered the geography, climate, history, connections with the Monarchy and culture of northern Thailand. His third chapter focussed on the fertility data for Chiangmai. In the supervisor's opinion, the first two chapters were dealing with materials which did not appropriately introduce the topic of the thesis; such materials might only be relevant at a later stage if they could be used to interpret the data on fertility. The student, however, explained that he considered it would be improper to start so abruptly on the main focus of his research—the purpose of the introduction in a thesis was to start slowly and on a very broad base and then gradually draw the reader's attention to the actual topic. This student knew that a thesis should have an introduction, a section on data, an analysis, and a discussion leading to a conclusion—but what the introduction should consist of was a culturally-determined matter. Once he had looked at a couple of completed PhD theses on related topics and had analysed the function of each section in the opening chapters, he was quite able to rework his material to the satisfaction of his supervisor.

Other examples abound which display a similar pattern: academic success in the home culture, failure in the new context of a western university, intervention by an adviser who identified the problem as one of cultural dislocation rather than linguistic incompetence, and thereafter a rapid—sometimes spectacular—regaining of competence. Just how swift this re-assumption of competence can be is illustrated by the case of an Indonesian MA student whose first draft chapter on Indonesian short stories was rejected by her supervisor in the most crushing terms: "So far below standard that it could have been written by a high school student". Yet this student was a university lecturer in her own country where her previous literary writing—essentially detailed summary with lengthy quotations—had been regarded as first-class. Her problem, it transpired, was not 'writing' but writing literary criticism using the appropriate (culturally determined) critical and analytical style. An examination of an article by a western critic on a similar subject was sufficient to enable her to recognize the analytical shift that was required—and to proceed to produce it in her next draft most competently. "I now see I have to ask questions," she said. "Before, all I did was admire the stories. I'm only just beginning to understand what questions I should ask, but I'm learning how to think, really. Like an Australian lecturer, I suppose."

4. Conclusion

The common thread running through all the work we do with students, whether Australian or overseas, whether undergraduate or postgraduate, is the recognition that successful academic writing is related to cultural adjustment. We approach student writing as an integrated process involving reading, note-taking, planning and writing, and as a process which can most effectively be acquired in the context of the academic demands each student is currently facing. Instruction in grammar or in ideal structures for essays, especially in isolation from the specific context, content and purpose of a particular essay and course, seems to be of marginal value. Students with competent English and an adequate formal structure for their writing are still in difficulty if they are approaching their materials in a manner inappropriate to the academic culture of which they are a part.

References

BALLARD, B. 'Language is not enough—Responses to the academic difficulties of overseas students', in Bock, H. and Gassin, J. (eds.) *Communication at University* (conference papers), La Trobe University, pp. 116–128, 1982.

BOCK, H. 'University essays as cultural battlegrounds—The problems of migrant students', in *Communication at University*, pp. 140–155, 1982.

CLANCHY, J. "'The Higher Illiteracy': Some personal observations", *English in Australia*, **37**, 20–24, 1976.

CLANCHY, J. 'Language in the university', *Education News*, **16**, 20–23, 1978.

CLANCHY, J. 'From school to university: The transition between two cultures', *English in Australia*, **56**, 15–24, 1981.

CLANCHY, J. and BALLARD, B. *Essay Writing for Students*, Melbourne: Longman Cheshire, 1981.

TAYLOR, G. 'Coming to terms with English Expression in the university', *Vestes*, **21**, 34–37, 1978.

Editor's Comment

This impressive paper neatly spans both sides of 'Communication in English' work. Ballard first discusses with considerable educational insight the *culture shift* that native speakers need to make on entering 'University culture' and then goes on to describe the *double culture shift* that faces many non-native speakers (cf. the paper by James); and, further, within this cultural orientation, she is fully aware of the particular requirements of disciplinary sub-cultures. Ballard thus exemplifies the imaginative and dedicated response of the Communication and Study Skills Unit at the Australian National University to the problems of both native speaker and non-native speaker students. The paper also therefore serves as an introduction to Australian activity in the field, and the select list of Australian references allows the reader to follow up this work if he or she should wish to do so.

JMS

WRITING TEXTS: COHESION IN SCIENTIFIC AND TECHNICAL WRITING

JUSTINE COUPLAND

University of Wales Institute of Science and Technology

Introduction

It is undeniably true that many students of science and engineering display a certain lack of competence when producing the sort of texts that are central to their disciplines—texts meant to fulfil the functions of describing, evaluating, summarizing, drawing inferences, recommending etc. Many of my own students express and demonstrate their own feelings of inadequacy in this respect when faced with a blank sheet of paper and armed only with rough notes, a pile of relevant literature, and some ideas that are still being formed. Part of the problem is that students of science and engineering have been encouraged during their training to think and write according to certain well-specified rules. The restricting conventions governing format and expression in the experimental report are a good example of this, where the writing task can easily be perceived as slotting in facts, theories, observations or conclusions into an existing framework. It is not surprising, then, that first-year undergraduates' modes of expression already tend to be moulded into a pattern, and that writing texts which do not conform to known genres is particularly problematical for them.

At UWIST, Communication Studies courses usually begin with a look at the process of communication, and at how language varies according to situation. One exercise commonly set is to evaluate a communication model in a small tutorial group, and then to write a short description (a page or two at most) of how the model can be applied to an everyday situation—television advertising, telling a joke, listening to a lecture etc. On the surface, this does not seem a particularly demanding writing task, but students' reactions and their answers show clearly that many find difficulty in synthesizing their ideas and making them succeed as *texts*. In fact, their answers make great demands on me, as reader, in having to actively and consciously construct links between ideas and arguments—links that are not formally represented in the texts themselves. Moreover, students sometimes fail to see the need to provide the information the reader needs to 'bridge the gaps' between sentences. The propositional development of an argument is incomplete through absence of what Nash (1980:21) calls 'overt marking of transition' or 'directive clues'. And as Nash comments "there are countless instances in the making of prose where the clarity of the text . . . (is) . . .

55

affected by the absence of such connectives". Foreign language students in CS classes may show that they are not aware of the meaning of sentence connectors, for example using *thus* when *nevertheless* is meant; but the absence or inappropriate use of such signalling devices is common to first as well as second language users. This is , of course, what we must expect, given that there are no hard and fast rules governing the extent to which sentences must be 'texturalized' in written English discourse. This is a general point recognized by Halliday and Hasan (1976:1): "The distinction between a text and a collection of sentences is in the last resort a matter of degree".

1.   The Importance of Textual Competence in Writing

All this points to a need to concentrate on something we might call (after Fowler, 1981:64) *textual competence* when developing materials for teaching writing skills. As far as I am aware, communication skills (CS) teachers ignore this need, although it is acknowledged by teachers of English as a foreign language (EFL) and English for specific purposes (ESP). We tend to assume that native speakers have, by the time they reach further/higher education, developed the skills necessary to write texts, and therefore that our energies as teachers should be directed towards specific, more tangible aspects of style and readability. This normally results in discussion of linguistic factors below the sentence level: vocabulary and jargon, nominal and verbal groups, sentence length and complexity. But as Widdowson (1979, 1980) points out of EFL (and I think it equally true of native English speakers) "a knowledge of how the language functions in communication does not necessarily follow from a knowledge of sentences". At least as important, then, is teaching student-writers to build textual entities out of individual sentences, and this can be presented as just another aspect of considering our audience's needs, which already plays a key role in most CS and Technical Writing Courses. After all, the extent to which the reader perceives the text as coherent and manageable is, as with all aspects of writing, the writer's responsibility.

2.   The Components of Textual Competence

In trying to define textual competence, we can point to two complementary aspects of textuality: cohesion and coherence. *Cohesion* refers to the formal, surface syntactic and semantic signals which link sentences within a text; *coherence* refers to the underlying relations between propositions. If we can make sense of a text, this is because we can perceive its coherence which will be indicated in part through cohesive devices—reference, substitution, ellipsis, and conjunction (cf. Halliday and Hasan, 1976). Widdowson explains the distinction as follows:

"Cohesion . . . is the overt relationship between propositions expressed through sentences. Where we recognise that there is a relationship between the illocutionary acts propositions, not always overtly linked, are being used to perform, then we are perceiving the coherence of a discourse" (1976:28).

In a similar way, de Beaugrande and Dressler (1981:3) talk of cohesion in terms of the components of the surface text which are mutually connected within a sequence, and of coherence as the configuration of concepts and relations underlying the surface. It is the insufficient or inappropriate use, then, of cohesive devices that often tends to reduce the coherence of students' texts. Widdowson again (1978:26)

"the difficulty we have in recovering propositional development is a measure of the degree of cohesion exhibited by a particular discourse. The difficulty might arise because the form of a sentence represents an inappropriate arrangement of information in respect to what has preceded: the work we have to do in making the necessary readjustment disturbs the propositional development, and to this extent impairs effective communication".

Shortly, I shall give examples of precisely this sort of difficulty in science and engineering students' writing, and suggest methods that may be able to develop sensitivity to coherence and cohesion. Before this, however, it is important to point out that the relationship between cohesion, propositional development and readability is not a simple one. It may be generally true to say that students who do not seem to have achieved an adequate level of textual competence err on the side of inexplicitness so that the teacher is generally having to encourage more use of cohesive links. But there is clearly an optimum level of explicitness beyond which a text becomes annoyingly redundant, for example with repetition of full nominals in subject and object positions (where pro-forms would have been more appropriate and comfortable to read). Also, contextual factors are vital in determining the appropriate extent and type of cohesive marking. de Beaugrande and Dressler have isolated what they call 'standards of textuality' over and above cohesion and coherence which affect writers' and readers' perceptions of appropriateness in a text. For example, *acceptability*: the suggestion here is that in different contexts, readers will accept different levels of cohesion and coherence. For example, certain texts require important contributions from the reader in order to be perceived as coherent. We read advertisements which are composed of superficially unrelated propositions, and find it entirely acceptable to expend effort filling in the semantic gaps. For the transmission of scientific and technical information, where the function of the text is generally an informative one, a more overt marking of relationships is generally taken to be appropriate. Again, de Beaugrande and Dressler talk of *informativity*, more commonly referred to as the unloading rate of a text. We can assume that the higher the informativity of a text, the greater will be the need for a well-developed network of cohesive links. A third contextual factor is *intertextuality* which refers to the factors which make the use of one text dependent upon knowledge of one or more previously encountered texts. In a scientific report, the transition between a Conclusions section and the Recommendations may need little cohesive marking, because of readers' familiarity with the conventional disposition of information in such reports: recommendation sections rarely have to begin with *therefore, as a result, thus*, etc.

3. Typical Problems with Cohesion

These considerations show the difficulty involved in presenting students with clear-cut guidelines for their use of cohesion. Nevertheless, they also give some indication of the sort of explanation which may help students to understand what is appropriate in particular cases. In order to present some examples of the sorts of difficulty that students have with cohesion, I worked through a set of twenty 4th year undergraduate (native English speakers') Industrial Training Reports. Students had been asked to select one aspect of what they had been doing, and write a report either explaining an industrial process, describing a piece of machinery, or reporting on a project they had completed. Five extracts of the reports are reproduced below, each followed by what I saw as problems of cohesion. (Numbers have been added to the texts for ease of reference.)

1. Report: *'Pure Nickel Blank Production at the Royal Mint'*
    Section: Discussion — new subsection
    "This trial was carried out with annealing before welding. It may be possible to leave out this (1) stage of the process and obtain a saving in the conversion cost of the material. Figure 2 is a copy of the hardness against reduction graph for nickel 200c a commercially available nickel alloy of similar composition to the material we have been processing. From this (2) we can see that although the material is very hard, its rate of hardening is fairly gradual. Thus it (3) may be possible. A further trial would soon determine this feasibility."
    (1) It is not clear what the anaphoric *this* refers to, whether to annealing or welding or both. Contextual clues would probably point to *annealing* as the referent, though this could not be depended on.
    (2) On first reading, *this* might be taken to refer to the material, until the reader relates *see* to *Figure 2*.
    (3) Again, there are many possible referents for *it*, although the reader can with some effort recover *leave out . . . annealing* from 3 sentences previously. The reader has to rely on the parallel construction (*it may be possible*) to forge the link.

2. Report: *The Alfa Laval Oil Purifier*
    Section: Apparatus and Operation (beginning of section)
    "The centrifuge is driven by a 11.18 kW (shaft output) motor and the drive incorporates a centrifugal clutch. There are two gear-type pumps driven from the centrifuge (1) wormwheel shaft. One of the gear-type pumps driven from the purifier wormwheel shaft (2) pumps contaminated oil from the turbine main oil tank through the regenerative and hot water sections of the plate exchanger to the purifier. A strainer is fitted to this pump."
    (1) In the first few lines the style sets up an expectancy of a high frequency of explicit repetition (*centrifuge . . . centrifugal . . . centrifuge.*)

(2) This expectation is broken by the confusing shift to *purifier wormwheel shaft*, especially as this and *centrifugal wormwheel shaft* are in fact intended to refer to the same item. In general, the student does not seem to have the resources to achieve an appropriate balance of given-to-new information in technical description.

3. Report: *Cost Comparison of Rubber versus Nylon*
   Section: Current Production Methods
   "After the *mandrel* has been extruded it is then taken to *mandrel* preparation where it is checked. The current method for joining the *mandrel* is by means of crimping the wire through the *mandrel*. Once checked, prepared and McLubed *it* is then dispatched to the inners where it awaits hose production. The *mandrel* is now not handled until it reaches the test and eject area, where the *mandrel* is ejected into drums and taken back down for *mandrel* preparation . . ."
   There are clearly opportunities here for ellipsis and substitution which the student (except on one occasion out of seven) does not seem to have the confidence to use.

4. Report: *Installation of a Ladle Steelmaker*
   Section: Discussion
   "In order that the many departments involved in installing and commissioning the plant could work in unison a good communications system was necessary. (1) A complete set of drawings for the scheme were unavailable at the start of the installation exercise, without these drawings planning proved difficult . . ."
   (1) Here, a sentence connective would have avoided the leap in interpretation involved. *However, Unfortunately* or *As it was* would have provided the reader with a cohesive link.

5. Report: *Mechanical Agitator Shaft Design*
   Section: Discussion
   "After consultation with a design engineer it was concluded that since no alternative was to hand the existing shaft should be used. (1) Some recommendations can be made in order to reduce the stress in the shaft as much as possible".
   (1) A similar problem; here *Still, Nevertheless, All the same* could have been used to link two prepositionally disconnected sentences.

4. Improving Textual Competence

The problems raised by cohesion in these texts show some of the kinds of difficulty which poorly-cohesive writing causes. So what, then, is the best way to use cohesion in order to write readable, accessible texts? As I have already shown, this is not a straightforward matter. Still, there are some general observations which can inform our attempts to guide students' writing. Halliday and Hasan (1976) point out that the most often used, and the simplest form of cohesion is anaphora. Since all too often this basic cohesive tie is not forged, it is as well to start by pointing out to students the fundamental contribution that anaphora makes to textuality—particularly through repetition and substitution. Only once the need for unambiguous reference has been established, is it feasible to go on to discuss the stylistic consequences of excessive repetition (see below). Cataphoric cohesion, which refers the reader forwards in the text, is the marked form and less frequently used across adjacent sentences. This type requires reading on before coherence can be established, and as readers we seem to find it an intrinsically more difficult procedure due to the memory load imposed as we hold, say, unexplicated pro-forms until their referents appear. (On the other hand, if we use the term cataphora to include global cohesive devices such as advance signalling (e.g. *Shortly I shall give examples of this kind of difficulty*), then cataphoric linkage can clearly be of considerable benefit to the reader of longer or more complex texts.)

Another significant aspect to be drawn to students' attention is the *distance* between cohesive ties. The greater the distance between cohesive ties, the more difficult for a reader to make semantic links and so perceive coherence in a text; and (conversely) the proximity of ties promotes readability because the search function is more easily and quickly performed.

A particular feature of scientific and technical texts, especially where a process is being explained or a piece of equipment described, is the frequent occurrence of chains of cohesive ties as small blocks of information are gradually pieced together into a whole. Students too often opt for the simplest solution—repetition—and need to be led to avoid heavily redundant texts by using pro-forms where necessary. Conjunction, which specifies the way in which what is to follow is connected to what has gone before, is a perennial problem and should be given some attention. It is relatively easy to persuade students of the importance of using sentence adverbials, but the global view of a text required to produce these appropriately is often missing. Often it is necessary to ask students to retrace the whole development of their argument in summary form, perhaps supported by schematic diagrams or plans.

It may well be that some types of discourse are more difficult to 'textualize' than others. Even within the industrial reports I surveyed, different textual functions seem to attract different sorts of problems of cohesion. Introductions and descriptions of machinery or experiments or procedures seem to cause fewer problems to the writer than later sections in the reports, where most of the factual content has already been put across, and deductions, inferences, conclusions and recommendations have to be made. Here, the logical progression of the writer's own thoughts and ideas have to be mapped on to a less well-defined structure, and there is more tendency for problems of cohesion to occur.

Finally, I should like to consider briefly some of the various ways in which we, as CS teachers, can set about improving the situation. Students obviously need to be made aware of their responsibilities as writers to use both local cohesion (across sentences) and global cohesion (in overall text structure) in a way which will enable readers to see their texts as coherent. The following sorts of exercise are suggestions for possible approaches.

1. Students are given a text jumbled as a random set of sentences which are to be organized into a coherent and cohesive text. Students are encouraged to respond to the linguistic features which mark cohesion, or rather those that will function as cohesive markers in the coherent text. The point to be made is that texts may be built up (both locally and globally) in a number of ways; different approaches should be looked at.

2. Students are given a set of very brief notes which they are asked to build into a text. Different versions may be compared, leading to discussion of points such as: conjunction, ellipsis, pro-forms, repetition, and how these are related to unloading rate and redundancy.

3. Students are asked
    a) to write a passage of description interpreting a labelled diagram or series of diagrams of a process or experiment; or
    b) to write a passage of interpretation of a graph or table, perhaps answering specific questions on the trends involved.
    A model text may be used in each case—in a) to give the original description, and in b) to give an example of interpretation. This can then be compared with students' own answers, and tactics discussed.

References

DE BEAUGRANDE, R. and DRESSLER, W. *Introduction to Text Linguistics*, London: Longman, 1981.
VAN DIJK, T. A. *Some Aspects of Text Grammars: a Study in Theoretical Linguistics and Poetics*, The Hague: Mouton, 1972.
FOWLER, R. *Literature as Social Discourse*, Batsford Academic, 1981.
HALLIDAY, M. A. K. and HASAN, R. *Cohesion in English*, London: Longman, 1976.
NASH, W. *Designs in Prose: a Study of Compositional Problems and Methods*, London: Longman, 1980.
WIDDOWSON, H. G. *Teaching Language as Communication*, Oxford: OUP, 1978.
WIDDOWSON, H. G. *Explorations in Applied Linguistics*, Oxford: OUP, 1979.

Editor's Comment

Coupland's paper is particularly useful for the ways in which it manages to apply recent studies of discourse (Halliday and Hasan, de Beaugrande and Dressler, Widdowson) to the teaching of scientific and technical writing. She rightly suggests that an informal approach to developing textual competence in Communication Skills writing courses has not always been apparent; and her paper thus usefully complements the more structural and cognitive approaches adopted by Ballard, Dudley-Evans and Swales, and derives support from and provides support to those sections of James' case-study that deal with 'faulty referencing' and 'weaknesses in signposting'.

JMS

STANDARDS OF WRITTEN EXPRESSION AMONG UNDERGRADUATES

PHILIP HOBSBAUM

University of Glasgow

1. The Decline of Literacy

We have been too complacent about the spread of popular education in the last century. More people can read and write than ever before, but they are doing so at a lower level. The standard of literacy among those deemed to be educated is worse than it was a hundred years ago. Students no longer come to university with a working knowledge of Latin and therefore tend not to understand the derivation of many words that they use. The result is a good deal of imprecise writing. The decline in the teaching of Latin has gone along with a decline in the teaching of grammar. This means that it is difficult now to explain to a student the nature of such mistakes as he makes in syntax. The modern student characteristically knows neither that the language has a structure nor that his departures from that structure are open to query and discussion. All this suggests that it is possible for a student to satisfy his assessors in public examinations and still come up to university gravely in need of basic tuition in language.

The process has been gradual for many years and has been substantially documented. One of the largest educational institutions in the UK is Glasgow University; by 1977, the standards of written expression among incoming students were noticeably shaky. At that point, however, there occurred a further, readily identifiable drop. In the Department of English Literature, which caters for most students in the Faculty of Arts, the number of first-year students who passed the Degree Examination taken at the end of the academic year 1977–78 went down by 10%. This decrease in the success rate has persisted, in spite of sporadic attempts to amend the standards. The finding in itself may not be conclusive. However, experience suggests that arts students characteristically fail, not through ignorance or stupidity, but because they are unable adequately to express that which they know. In other words, the basic reason for failure is a result of breakdown in written expression. A great deal of correspondence resulting from the publication of this finding suggests that Glasgow is not a special case, and that in the middle-to-late 1970s a series of factors (see Section 4 of this paper) combined to bring about the symptoms that are about to be identified (see Section 2).

This was not a malfunction characteristic of a single group of university subjects. Other faculties at Glasgow University were canvassed and they produced further evidence for concern. Students, it seemed, had become less able than their predecessors to write an essay in conceptual prose, to produce a report, to translate a foreign text into intelligible English, to describe an experiment, even—a point taken from the Department of Electrical Engineering—to write a précis.

A number of Glasgow academics, culled from all faculties, undertook a survey of written work done by students in the university. Most of these were examination scripts, and those conducting the survey were well aware that nobody writes at his best under examination conditions. However, until better conditions can be devised, these remain the norm of university procedure in assessing students. In any case, there was less difference than might have been supposed between scripts surveyed and the essays or reports done under conditions less exacting. A vast number of errors were extracted from the scripts, essays and reports under survey, and the types of error that seemed to predominate were selected and classified. The fact that these errors predominated means that they are representative and not extreme cases. The examples following represent the failures in written expression characteristic of the borderline pass or the borderline fail, where of course the problems of assessment tend to congregate. What we have here is the characteristic expression of a broad average of first-year students.

The problems identified mostly involve sentences which are poorly constructed. Defects of spelling, of vocabulary, of punctuation, mostly attend upon problems of construction. A mode of classification was developed based upon analysis of these characteristic examples. Eight basic modes of error were identified. Mostly they involved mistakes in grammar. However, since the classification was based upon the practical writing of English prose, it proved impossible to isolate grammar from style, or logic from either. Therefore the system of classification, as well as identifying grammatical misconstructions, involves elements of stylistic clumsiness and of logical blur. This mode of classification has been accepted by those to whom it has been made known, and therefore it has been retained in the following survey of basic misconstructions in student writing.

2. Student Writing: Solecisms, Analyses, Fair Copies

2.1 The Crocodile Sentence

The Crocodile Sentence is one of the most predominant of all *solecisms*, as the mistakes students repetitiously make will be termed. It is the sentence that never seems to end—which goes on, through floating participles and tenuously related clauses, with regard to neither grammar nor logic. One symptom is a subject imperfectly signified or out of control. For the purpose of classification and comparison, an example will be put forward, together with an analysis to indicate nature of breakdown; and this will be followed by a suggested revision which will be termed a *fair copy*.

On Hamlet

Let || represent the end of what may be deemed either an independent clause or the raw material for one.

A
The audience at this time are totally involved in the play ||
B
and see the fact that Claudius admits to the murder and that Hamlet hears him as very dramatic in its action ||,
C
they believe that this will be the end of Claudius ||,
D
however, they are lulled into deception ||
F
and receive even greater dramatic interest ||
E
when Hamlet decides that this is not the time to kill the king ||,
E
later if it is possible ||.

Fair Copy

The audience by this time are deeply involved in the drama. They see Claudius admit the murder in Horatio's hearing and, quite naturally, believe that such an admission would destroy Claudius for ever. However, any conjectures of this nature would be quite mistaken. Hamlet sees that this is not the time to kill the king and decides, if possible, to defer his vengeance. This delay in the action seems to raise the dramatic tension even higher.

2.2   The Incomplete 'Sentence'

The Incomplete 'Sentence' is not a sentence at all; that is why the noun here is in inverted commas. Such a 'sentence' usually lacks a subject or a verb phrase (here termed a *predicator*), or both. This means the sentence fails to make sense or, at best, leaves a good deal to be inferred by the reader. Sometimes this solecism is taken to be an error in punctuation, but the effect is more disabling than this would suggest. When the incidence of solecism is doubled and redoubled throughout an examination paper, the whole is reduced to the semblance of rough notes.

On Hamlet

In the prayer scene Hamlet knows if he doesn't act now he may never have another chance. Yet he wants his revenge proper. To kill the body and send the soul to hell.

It is the last 'sentence' that is in question, and two possible analyses suggest themselves. The first possibility is that the subject and the predicator have been omitted. In such a case the 'sentence' consists only of a complement —

S	P	C
⋏	⋏	to kill the body and send the soul to hell.

The other possibility is that the 'sentence' consists only of a subject. In that case, it would be the predicator, along with the complement, that is omitted —

S		P	C
To kill the body and send the soul to hell		⋏	⋏ .

Any fair copy of this solecism, if it is to be intelligible, will necessarily involve a considerable expansion of the original.

Fair Copy

The prayer scene offers Hamlet what may be his only chance to kill the King, and Hamlet knows this. Yet he wants his revenge to be as complete as possible. He wishes not only to kill the King but to kill him in such circumstances as will ensure that his soul goes to hell.

2.3   Fragmentation

Fragmentation occurs when the various parts of the sentence — subject (S), predicator (P), complement (C), adjunct (A), qualifier (Q) — fail to relate to one another. The result can be obscurity, uncontrolled ambiguity, or undue repetition. As with previous classifications and examples, failure comes about as a result of the subject controlling the author rather than the author the subject.

On 'The Collar' by George Herbert

He asks that after all his work is all that he obtains discontment [*sic*], can he not have something to restore the love that he once had for the church.

Basically this sentence consists of two independent clauses (α and α), each of which has a subject ('he') identical with that of the other. That subject, however, is inconclusively signified in the first clause, which is really about work and discontent. Though both independent clauses add up to a statement, the second clause has a form normally associated with a question. That is to say, it begins with a predicator split by the subject — 'can he not have . . .' — and this, given the context, is clumsy and makes for confusion.

α

S	P	C
He |	asks	[[that | after all his work | is | all that he obtains | discontment]] ||,

and α

| P – | S | – P | C | Q |

can <he> not have | something [to restore the love [[he once had for the church]]]||.

Fair Copy

Apparently, after his work, all he finds is discontent. He asks, therefore, whether the love that he once had for the church can be restored.

2.4 Linguistic Displacement

Linguistic Displacement is the use of a word in the wrong sense. Characteristically it arises from a misapprehension of fact; it is seldom that the misplaced word betokens merely a linguistic error. Usually its occurrence suggests that there has been a misunderstanding at a deeper level than that of the unintentional substitution of one word for another.

On Byron

Byron's chief models for satire were the Lake Poets, especially Wordsworth.

Apparent Meaning

Byron went to the tattling of Wordsworth's villagers in *Lyrical Ballads* in order to learn how to pillory, in *Don Juan*, the sophisticated vices of London society.

Displacement

'models' for 'topics'

Fair Copy

Byron's chief topics for satire were the Lake Poets, especially Wordsworth. NB Not true

2.5 False Statement of Equivalence

False Statement of Equivalence often looks like a logical error. It is, however, usually a result of sloppiness in prose, e.g. confusion of tense, or identification with one another of entities which are disparate. It is in practice easy to see why this solecism is sometimes called an error of content. One frequent symptom is the omitted link.

On Rob Roy by Sir Walter Scott

The main theme of *Rob Roy* is to my mind *Romance* ⅄ but it is so *underplayed* as ⅄ to *forget it is there*.

The italicized words represent over-simplification: 'main theme' is not equivalent to 'Romance', and 'underplayed' is not equivalent to 'forget it is there'. Omitted links, signified by ⅄, include 'depiction of Romance' and the subject of the verbal group 'to forget'—i.e. *who* forgets it is there? Once more, in revising an unsatisfactory original, it is necessary to add a good deal to the sense.

Fair Copy

Rob Roy is, in content and form, a Romance. But its qualities of beauty and strangeness are not taken to extremes. Rather they tincture the book and lend it atmosphere.

2.6   Heavy Metaphor

The main trouble with Heavy Metaphor is that what should be taken as defining or illustrating some central statement tends to emerge as literal fact and/or a statement in its own right. In the following example it causes Claudius to assume the colour of Othello.

On Hamlet

It is, however, true that Claudius is here seen as a man very black but it is his own words that paint him black.

'Seen', 'paint' and the second occurrence of 'black' are words that obtrude unnecessarily. Further, there is an omitted link: after the word 'but', some reason for the observation should have been given.

Fair Copy

It is, however, true that Claudius is represented at this point in the play as a man black with sin, but this is a result of no authorial bias: he is condemned in the end by his own words.

2.7   Trailing Off

Trailing off is a fault of style rather than syntax. The sentence droops when it has run out of subject, and still dribbles on. One key characteristic is that the various components of the sentence appear in no significant order, and so any sense of emphasis is lost. Quite often the components occurring late in the sentence are unnecessary to the meaning, and so one has a sense of anticlimax.

On Waiting for Godot by Samuel Beckett

Vladimir needs Estragon in order to give him some sort of footing in the world to recognize the setting and to give him someone to enact verbal games with.

Fair Copy

Vladimir needs Estragon as a partner in verbal games and as a help to establishing a context for himself; and in this way he maintains a precarious foothold on the world.

2.8 Vagueness

This often occurs, paradoxically, when the student is trying to identify a quality or define a characteristic in the topic he is discussing. In practice the effect is often that of a sentence starting before its subject comes into existence. It is a way of saying nothing while giving an impression of saying something. Out of context it tends to look as though it refers to a context. In context all too often it is itself a referent.

On George Herbert

Herbert employs the use of appropriate metaphor.

Here there is redundancy: one would say either 'employ' or 'use', not both. There is also an omission: what is the metaphor 'appropriate' to?

Fair Copy

It is impossible to produce a fair copy. The sentence says nothing and therefore cannot be rewritten.

3. English Across the Curriculum

The examples so far are drawn from students reading English literature. It might be said that the topics that concern that subject might bring out special modes of written error. But concern about written prose has nothing to do with topic: it is spread throughout the university. It is not, however, evenly distributed. Difficult languages, such as Greek and Hebrew, tend to be taken only by those who already have a high degree of literacy in English. Certain medical subjects require little in the way of discursive writing from their students. But in the main there is a surprising cohesion among the disciplines so far as student writing is concerned. It has been possible to identify the same categories of error in those ostensibly engaged in quite different areas of study. A Crocodile Sentence is a Crocodile Sentence, irrespective of the topic it seeks to discuss. For example:

"Drivers tend to take about two-thirds of a curve as transitional from studies carried out thus they would not be using parts of the transitions as they would be driving round them as a surcular [sic] curve they also tend to cut corners so they would dirve [sic] straight when curve was changing from left hand curve to a right hand curve thus not using the transitions" (Civil Engineering).

"This leads to the problem of whether or not an action could be thought of as not instinctive just because under some extreme condition it was influenced by the environment i.e. Whether we should take an action to be instinctive only if it is unchanging through all the possible different environments, or if we could allow a certain fluctuation in the action and still call it instinctive" (Zoology).

By now the diagnosis should be apparent. Something has gone wrong with the way in which students express themselves, and this is to a great extent independent of their area of study. To be wholly certain of this ground a group would have to be formed capable of assessing the prose of every script written in every university over a period of years. Here it is only necessary to say that further investigation seems to be required. But it would be impossible to develop such a study without seeking to envisage, alongside the description of decline, some reasons as to why the decline has taken place. The propositions that follow should be taken not as incontrovertible statements, but as invitations to debate.

4. Fourteen Theses

1. There has been a gradual decline in literacy in groups hitherto deemed to be literate. This has taken place during the last hundred years. Our own century has been marked by the gradual abandonment of Latin and of English grammar as areas of study in schools. The two facts, of decline and of abandonment, may be related.

2. The last generation of Latinists and grammarians, but for a few stragglers, has already retired. If it is agreed that this may have conduced to a decline in literacy, then it is probable that a great many of our English teachers in schools at present are not wholly conversant with their area of study. This may in part account for the acceleration of the decline in recent years.

3. Another differentiating factor between the present and the past is that over the last twenty years an increasing number of children have gone to comprehensive schools: that is to say, schools that are non-selective. This is not the only factor causing a decline in literacy; it may not even be the prime factor; but it must be taken as one of the possible factors in the decline, if it is not to be written off as a genial coincidence.

4. In many comprehensive schools and possibly in most, streaming has been

abandoned over considerable portions of the courses. In the West of Scotland, for example, a considerable number of comprehensive schools go in for mixed ability teaching in the first two years of secondary education. In certain quarters this has become an educational fetish, betokening a notion of equality. Yet, in a mixed group, pupils of advanced attainment are held back, while pupils of less advanced attainment are confused by the mean rate of progress possible. Groups of mixed ability have increased in recent years, so has the rate of the decline in literacy among university entrants. If this is not a coincidence, it must be taken as a factor.

5. Less and less writing goes on in school. This is a fact that affects not only the study of English but that of history, modern languages and the sciences. More and more, notes are dictated; more and more, work sheets are distributed; more and more, weight is placed upon such ancillary devices of study as the cassette-recorder. The Scottish Council for Research in Education has a report, not published at the time the present paper was in preparation, called *Writing Across the Curriculum*. The forebodings of the early drafts are dire. Less and less writing is expected of school pupils, and there is no reason to suppose that conditions are more favourable in England and Wales than in Scotland.

6. More and more of what writing there is takes the shape, not of ordered essays and reports, but of notes and of the disbursement of such notes in the examination room. Whatever merit the taking and disbursement of notes may have as a learning process, it is counterproductive as regards prose composition. The probability is that notetaking and disbursement result in such solecisms as the Crocodile Sentence and Fragmentation.

7. More children than ever before are taking public examinations. This means that a great number of candidates are likely to do badly. There is a distinct possibility that the weight of poor candidates drags the standard down: no Chief Examiner wants to fail the bulk of candidates in any given year. It is useless to speak of the percentage of pupils gaining A-levels at any given standard if we do not have precise information about the relation of that standard to those of previous years. Such information could only be drawn from the publication of representative scripts at the main standards of performance year after year.

8. We have to remember that the number of pupils taking public examinations is far greater than the intake of our universities. What is a university's entire intake is only a proportion of those leaving school. The inference is that the later years of the school cannot be designed for the university candidate. The university candidate, therefore, may not be adequately trained for university.

9. We cannot rely on the public examinations sorting out the students of greatest ability or even (so far as the university is concerned) of highest

attainment. Many of the qualities singled out by the public examinations are irrelevant to the needs of the university. For example, at a recent conference (School-Universities Liaison Committee for the Teaching of English, Ross Priory, March 1982) it was clear that the Scottish Highers examiners favoured poetic prose over the prose of reportage. Such a preference would certainly influence teachers preparing pupils for Scottish Highers.

10. There is a hiatus between the education of the pupil leaving school and that which he gets when he enters university. Any first-year tutor knows this; but those who design educational policy are seldom first-year tutors. The growing stratum of sixth-form colleges and colleges of further education suggests that some students and teachers recognize the existence of this hiatus. But it is not widely agreed that such halfway houses are the best way of filling it. In any case, sixth-form colleges are unevenly distributed.

11. We cannot rely on the universities as at present constituted to bridge the hiatus between themselves and the schools. Academics are primarily concerned with their own areas of study and have little time to assess English prose composition. The student will be penalized if he cannot write coherently under examination conditions; yet his previous circumstances of education may well be such as to have protected him from ever finding out what coherent expression entails. It is arguable that many students fail because their inexperience does not meet the relatively sophisticated demands of the university. It is certainly true that increasingly, whether they pass or fail, students feel themselves to be under a strain. One growth industry is that of the student medical officer, welfare worker and faculty adviser. Students who have never been taught to write ordered prose are expected to write ordered prose at university, and the university makes no provision for this.

12. The problem is not simply educational; no educational problem simply is. There is a crisis of morale among teachers in the state system which can be characterized by pointing at the current amount of absenteeism. It is impossible to find out how much of this is caused by genuine illness, and this must be admitted as the most impressionistic of the propositions here set forth. Yet parents and teachers alike may feel themselves to be aware of a rise in staff absences in the last ten years. A related phenomenon is the increase in administrative and other non-pedagogical duties undertaken by senior staff, rendering their presence increasingly intermittent in the classroom.

13. Children are now subject to distractions that did not exist in former days. A present-day pupil, tired of study, will seek relief in television. In effect, two hours a day that could have been spent in study or recreation go into the box; we shall be fortunate if it is not more. The book has been displaced from its position of centrality in our culture; reading is now a special event. This means that students taking university courses are being determined culturally in a way quite distinct from the middle-aged educationists who designed those courses.

14. Many young people feel that there is a crisis of morale in their peer-group. Some admit this crisis in themselves and most will be found to recognize it in others: "They don't work because they feel there's no hope. It's all pointless; there is nothing for them to look forward to". The present state of unemployment among the young is hardly conducive to an atmosphere of study. Some students at university give the impression of being there as an alternative to the dole. Even those with morale enough to aim for a reasonable class of degree know perfectly well that there is no guarantee of employment after they graduate.

5.   Conclusion: A Place for Writing

The conclusion of all this is that universities are accepting students at a level of literacy that would not have been permitted as recently as ten years ago. Whatever the strain on their resources, universities will have to assume a responsibility which used to be that of the schools. A student who has not been given practice in writing before reaching university must be given such practice at the university.

This is how it can be done. Students with linguistic problems recognized by their subject tutors should be referred to a central unit catering for students of all faculties. The unit should be manned by staff with interests and skills related to teaching composition. If necessary, the unit should be staffed on a rota system so that most teachers with the necessary capabilities get a chance to help students with difficulties, while no teacher finds himself confined to that one sector of tuition. Then the education of those whose linguistic attainment is low could proceed coherently, rather than (as at present) piecemeal or not at all. A great deal of the educational process in this area of composition is a matter of re-orientation and increase in the capacity for self-criticism. One tries, in practice, to inculcate in the student the sensation of a reader over his shoulder. Many of the most frequent faults in writing are obvious, and they tend to disappear after they are pointed out. It is hard for faults to stand up against cogent explanation. No doubt techniques of greater sophistication than those used in such composition courses as currently exist would evolve with practice. But we cannot ignore the problem. It will not go away.

The researches of the Literacy Group at Glasgow University suggested that those requiring a great deal of help with their English amounted to as many as 10% of the first-year intake. That is something like 170 students every year. This opinion is buttressed by many sources of information. The *New Civil Engineer*, the magazine of the Institute of Civil Engineers, wrote in its issue of 30.4.81 that the failure rate in the Professional Examination for chartered status had risen to 25%, and commented: "Nearly one third of all who failed . . . did so solely because they were incapable of writing a simple essay with clarity and good grammar". These figures refer to graduates throughout the United Kingdom.

We have a problem. If we think it will go away of its own accord, we shall have a crisis. We are about to go below the minimum number of highly literate people required to keep our communication base valid. If matters get worse, we shall not have sufficient people literate enough to impart the communication skills which previous generations took for granted among educated people. Some critics would even argue that the communication base has deteriorated beyond recall, that with the retirement of the Latinists and the grammarians, our present-day teachers do not have command over the areas they teach.

What is also disturbing is that there has been no efflorescence of high literacy to counterbalance the decline which has been the subject of this paper. We would be hard put to indicate any recent equivalent to Mill, Ruskin, Newman or Morris. There is not even an equivalent to Shaw, Russell or Leavis.

It is true that, in the heyday of the Victorian age, fewer people were able to write. But, in our day, more lies within the public sector: we depend far more on ordered information, on reports, on a pool of communication skills.

That pool is being depleted. It is depleted by the loss of crucial subject areas in schools, by potentially talented schoolchildren lost in groups of mixed ability. It is depleted by teacher absenteeism, by falling and increasingly irrelevant examination standards, by social (or rather anti-social) distractions, by educational dislocation as our pupils pass from school to university, by the failure of universities to recognize that dislocation, by a public indifference attributable in no small degree to cynicism in high places.

Our students are no less intelligent than their predecessors. They are, however, less knowledgeable and less skilled. If we are teachers, we will help them in their difficulties. But, to do this, we must be able to adapt ourselves to new processes. In particular, we shall need to reorient certain procedures in the university. It was always a place of reading; but, if it is to remain a central forum with a social function in the world, the university must be henceforward primarily a place for writing.

References

BIAGGINI, E. *The Reading and Writing of English*, London: Hutchinson Scientific, 1936.
COX, C. B. *Education: The Next Decade, Conservative Political Centre*, 1981.
GREEN, G. Kenneth 'Why Comprehensives Fail', in *Black Paper 1975*, ed. Cox, C. B. and Boyson Rhodes, London: Dent, 1975.
HOBSBAUM, Philip, KAY, Christian, MILNE, Robin, HEWITT, R. H. *et al.*, *Report to the Senate from Glasgow University Literacy Group*, Glasgow University Literacy Group, 1981.
KNIGHTS, L. C. 'A Scrutiny of Examinations', *Scrutiny*, 1933–34.
LEAVIS, F. R. and THOMPSON, Denys *Culture and Environment*, London: Chatto and Windus, 1933.
ORWELL, George 'Politics and the English Language', in *Selected Essays*, Harmondsworth: Penguin, 1957.

SPENCER, Ernest 'Copying Across the Curriculum', *Teaching English*, Spring 1981.

Editor's Comment

We are accustomed to regarding communication breakdown as existing primarily in science and technology. In the L2 situation, the seemingly never-ending stream of published textbooks in all branches of EST is evidence of the need. And in the L1 situation, professional bodies such as the UK Council of Engineering Institutions make annual pleas for greater attention to be paid to standards of written expression. It is therefore particularly interesting to note, in Philip Hobsbaum's paper, that a sizeable proportion of L1 students of *English literature* at a major UK university also have unacceptable standards of written expression.

Philip Hobsbaum's proposed solution is almost identical to that currently being practised by Chris de Winter Hebron (this volume): namely, individual editorial guidance during the drafting process, emphasizing that the onus for reader-comprehension rests squarely on the writer.

Many British universities are, in recent years, becoming increasingly aware of inadequate standards of communication — some of their own volition, some at the insistence of professional institutions. But the provision of courses to improve L1 students' standards remains patchy: some (such as UWIST, Loughborough, Bristol) make specific provision, while others pretend the problem does not exist.

RCW

RESEARCH INTO THE STRUCTURE OF INTRODUCTIONS TO JOURNAL ARTICLES AND ITS APPLICATION TO THE TEACHING OF ACADEMIC WRITING

JOHN SWALES

University of Aston in Birmingham

Introduction

Since 1978 I have been offering courses in Report and Project Writing for overseas postgraduates, and over these years I have become particularly dissatisfied with the prescriptive and under-researched character of the Units dealing with the writing of *Introductions*. It seemed to me that in this aspect of English for Academic Purposes the quality of available materials (including my own) was in inverse proportion to their utility.

Useful teaching materials dealing with many of the central issues in Project Writing (such as *Describing Results*) certainly exist (Jordan, 1980, Dudley-Evans, 1981). However, it is precisely in areas such as these that the overseas postgraduate student or researcher has less need of our EAP assistance, for these are the areas that make less demand on his communicative competence as a writer. In contrast, it seemed to me, we were providing a poor service in the communicatively tricky areas such as *introducing the research topic* and *describing relevant previous research*. 'We looked with unconcern on a man struggling for life in the water, and when he reached ground, encumbered him with help.'

In one sense, it is not difficult to see why *Introductions to Journal Articles and Technical Reports* have suffered from ESP neglect. *Description of method* and the *writing up of results* are central and highly conventionalized products of a science education extending from Junior Secondary School to postgraduate study, and have, therefore, gained the attention of ESP teachers and textbook writers at all levels. Writing an introduction to an article is obviously a more specialized activity and has, as a result, a much lower market potential for the publisher. Further, it is much more difficult for the materials writer to extract and be confident about useful pedagogical generalizations in an introduction: the variability is so much greater because the communicative roles are so much more complex, and so much more variable from one *introduction* to another. And where generalizations have been offered, they tend not to be borne out in reality, such as the instruction 'begin with a statement of aim'.

But in another sense, this neglect is surprising. For one thing, there can be little doubt that English is consolidating its pre-eminence as the world's major language of scholarship. Although I have no reliable statistics about the proportion of scholarly journals published in English throughout the world, it is certainly remarkably high in some disciplines—a figure of 80% has been suggested for Engineering, for example. The higher such percentages, inevitably the greater is the number of papers being written by scholars who do not have English as a first language. (In my sample, as far as I can guess from name and place of work, about half of the authors are non-native speakers.) Secondly, there is much anecdotal evidence to suggest that nearly all writers have more difficulty with getting started on a piece of academic writing than with the later sections. The opening paragraph presents us with a wealth of options: we must decide how much background information to include; we must decide how far opposing views should be taken into account; and we must decide whether it is better to announce our conclusions and then justify them, or to lead the reader step by step, or to present a set of arguments and then destroy them (the 'straw-man' procedure).

Moreover, it is widely recognized that publications have a peculiarly important place in the academic world; they are 'rites of passage' along the road to professional advancement and promotion. Further, academics are no less inundated with paper than other professional groups, and the time they have for perusing the proliferating journals of their specialization is limited. Thus the abstract and introduction of a journal article must compete for the attention of a busy readership. I therefore feel there is a strong pedagogical justification for attempting to develop our understanding of the mechanics of writing the introduction of journal articles, because I assume that many overseas postgraduates, researchers and academics are facing up to the problems of writing articles in English and can be supposed, for the reasons I have outlined, to be having particular difficulty with the opening paragraphs. Many more are presumably *reading* scholarly journals.

If it appears that this aspect of academic writing has been neglected in EAP, it has certainly not been ignored in the vast literature (mainly American) aimed at helping native speakers with technical reports, theses, term papers and articles. However, the advice I have seen on *introductions* is at a level of rhetorical generality that makes it only partly helpful for the non-native speaker. A typical extract from one of the best-regarded British manuals (O'Connor and Woodford, 1976) must suffice:

The Introduction
"Make the introduction brief, remembering that you are not writing a review article: two or three paragraphs are usually enough. Indicate the aim and scope of the paper. State your purpose in undertaking the work and—in appropriate disciplines—where it was done. Explain how your investigation moves forward from closely related, previous work on the same subject. Be concise but clear: aim to waken interest rather than stifle it with fussy detail, and try to gain and keep the attention of readers who are not specialists in your field."

This is splendid advice, but hardly the stuff from which an EAP course can be directly fashioned.

1. Procedure

In the previous section I identified an 'EAP materials hole' and then tried to establish that its dimensions may be larger than might appear at first sight. In the remainder of this paper I would like to offer a commentary on my preliminary endeavours to fill this hole, and I raise the question of whether certain aspects of this enquiry might not have implications for first language work. Right from the outset I recognized that gaining even a modicum of insight into the rationale of article introductions was not going to be a simple task: for instance, my cursory readings of introductions had shown that this rationale is no straightforward matter of 'nods all round to previous researchers and then on with your own thing'. I concluded that some research would be necessary, probably of two kinds: a linguistic/discoursal examination of the Article-Introductions themselves and, subsequently, a series of interviews with researchers in order to discover something of the processes involved in their drafting of introductions.

It is obvious that an introduction can vary greatly in scale from a hundred-page survey in a PhD thesis to a single paragraph in a short article. Clearly, the provisional establishment of categories could proceed much faster if it were based on a larger number of short introductions rather than on a study of one or two extensive examples, so it was decided to limit the research to introductions to journal articles. In retrospect, this decision seems less easy to justify than it did originally. True, I could indeed look at quite a number of Article-Introductions and so hope for better-based generalizations than would otherwise have been the case—and also look for useful assistance for reading courses. But Article-Introductions were not perhaps ideal models for my clientele, partly because of the space constraints under which they are produced, and partly because they were examples of what my overseas postgraduates would hopefully be wanting to write in the future rather than what they needed to fulfil higher degree requirements.

We[1] also decided that we should attempt to cover a range of academic disciplines, particularly because I was interested in seeing whether or not Article-Introductions divided along subject-area lines. Clearly, any significant findings on this issue would have an influence on the appropriacy of offering advanced writing courses on a Departmental, on a Faculty or on a University-wide basis. The corpus therefore consisted of 48 recent Article-Introductions selected at random from three main areas: 16 from the 'hard' sciences, 16 from the biology/medicine field, and 16 from the social sciences (education, management and linguistics).

2. The Structure of Article-Introductions and the Signalling of Moves

So far a preliminary discourse analysis has been completed, and the second 'interview' stage is in hand. There is not space here to describe the findings in any detail, but I would like to outline three major, if tentative, conclusions.

The first refers to the discourse structure of Article-Introductions. As the research developed, there emerged a predominating structure for this type of introduction that occurred in over half the cases examined: this structure consists of four sequenced moves. With the exception of move 2, the moves need to be clearly signalled to the reader. In moves 3 and 4 this signalling optimally occurs at the beginning of the stretch of text articulating that move, whereas in the opening section, certain prefacing or preparatory material can initially occur. The broadest outlines of the structure are given in Figure 1.

MOVE ONE	*Establishing the Field* a) by asserting centrality OR b) by stating current knowledge
MOVE TWO	*Summarizing Previous Research*[2]
MOVE THREE	*Preparing for Present Research* a) by indicating a gap in previous research OR b) by raising a question about previous research
MOVE FOUR	*Introducing the Present Research* a) by stating the purpose OR b) by outlining present research

Figure 1

This overall pattern is now illustrated with two introductions, the first specially constructed (Figure 2), the second taken from *Language*, Volume 54 (Figure 3).

MOVE ONE (*Establishing the Field*)	There is reason to believe that most writers (both native and non-native speakers of English) have particular difficulty when constructing the opening paragraphs of their papers and articles. Therefore, 'insight' into the structure of Article-Introductions would potentially be of considerable pedagogical and instructional benefit.
MOVE TWO (*Summarizing previous Research*)	Previous research has largely concentrated on specific features of Article-Introductions: Oster (1981) examined tense-sequence in engineering articles, Dubois (1981) demonstrated the developing elaboration of key noun-phrases in biomedical journal introductions, and evidence of the above-average occurrence of *that-nominal* constructions in literature survey sections has been reported (West, 1980). The only description in the literature of a 'generalized plot' is of the problem-solution type (Hepworth, 1978).

MOVE THREE *(Preparing for Present Research)*	However, with the possible exception of Hepworth, all these studies have been based on a very small number of texts.
MOVE FOUR *(Introducing Present Research)*	The aim of this paper is to describe a relatively frequent four-part schema for Article-Introductions derived from a sizeable corpus of material.

Figure 2

The above introduction opens with what I have called *Field-establishment*: that is, the author attempts to establish that the field of research he is working in is of some significance, and that the research he is going to describe is useful, relevant, or important in some way or ways. (As Figure 1 indicates, he *could* have begun by referring to the state of current knowledge — "Relatively little is known at the moment about the discourse-structure of Article-Introductions".) The writer then proceeds to summarize previous research. There appear to be three main possibilities here. One option is to relate the history by describing what previous researchers have found, reported, demonstrated, suggested, etc. This *central-reporting* option has been chosen for the references to Oster and Dubois, where the authors cited occupy prominent subject-positions in their clauses. Alternatively, the writer can maintain an essentially *reporting* orientation but place the authors cited in brackets (i.e. *parenthetical reporting*), as is the case with West. Finally, he may adopt a *non-reporting* style, stating the findings or hypotheses as simple or qualified results, as happened with the Hepworth reference. (The reader may have noticed that option-choice appears to be a strong determinant of tense — a finding that will be taken up in the concluding section.)

The article-writer now has to establish that the previous research history is not complete, i.e. there are aspects of the research field still deserving of further enquiry. Apparently, the most common way of achieving this is to offer a negative evaluation of some feature of MOVE TWO, either by indicating some gap in research or knowledge, or by raising a question. As might be expected, the feature selected is then picked up in the fourth move as a prominent feature of the research about to be reported, MOVE THREE thus forming a bridge between previous research and the current research described in the rest of the article.

The 'real' introduction now follows (Figure 3), deliberately taken from the field of linguistics.

MOVE ONE	1. INTRODUCTION. An elaborate system of marking social distance and respect is found in the morphology of Nahuatl as spoken in communities of the Malinche volcano area in the Mexican states of Tlaxcala and Puebla. The complexity of the morphology involved, the semantic range of the elements, and variation in the system in use raise questions of considerable interest for our understanding of the form and function of such systems, both in Nahuatl itself and in other languages.

MOVE TWO   A system of elements usually referred to as 'honorifics' or 'reverentials' is
             reported by all the grammarians of Classical Nahuatl (cf. Olmos, 1547;
             Molina, 1571a; Carochi, 1645; Simeon, 1885; Garibay, 1970; Anderson,
             1973; Andrews, 1975). Similar systems are reported for several modern
             varieties of Nahuatl (cf. Whorf, 1946 for Milpa Alta in the Federal District;
             Pittman, 1948 for Tetelcingo in Morelos; and Buchler and Freeze, 1966 and
             Buchler, 1967 for Hueyapan and Atempan in northern Puebla).

MOVE THREE   None of these reports, except for Pittman's, describes the system in much
             detail.

MOVE FOUR   The present account is based on materials collected in 1974–75 and during
             the summer of 1976 in a linguistic survey of Nahuatl-speaking communities
             on the western and south-western slopes of the Malinche volcano.

Figure 3

We can see in this case that the opening sentence is not a *field-establishment*; indeed, it is likely to be a 'turn-off' for any reader without a specialist interest in Nahuatl. It is the second sentence which establishes the field, by the appeal to the readership contained in "raise questions of *considerable interest* for our understanding of the form and function of such systems, both in Nahuatl itself and *in other languages*". The rest of the introduction follows the four-move pattern. In the final move the authors do not directly state that they will be offering a highly-detailed description of the phenomena under scrutiny, but I think the reader will make this assumption from the reference to "materials collected in 1974–75 and during the summer of 1976".

3.   The Article-Introduction as an Exercise in Public Relations

The second main conclusion I would like to draw from the linguistic research stage of this materials development project is already implicit in the commentaries on the two introductions discussed so far. There is a tendency to believe — and this tendency is greatly reinforced by all the technical manuals on the writing of scholarly works — that writing an introduction is an activity totally governed by objectivity and reason, and devoted to straight reportage of previous research and judicious appraisal of the place and merit of the writer's own research. However, the more I have examined Article-Introductions from a range of fields, the more I have become convinced that this belief is a polite fiction. It seems to me that many Article-Introductions are essentially exercises in public relations. On the surface, they may indeed be instances of problem-solution text types, but beneath that surface they are *pleas* for acceptance, and designed accordingly.

The most useful way of characterizing this role that I can think of is to adopt the Conversation Analysts' concept of 'second-storying'. We know from everyday experience that if somebody tells a story or relates an anecdote in a conversational group, then at the closure of the story, one standard way of continuing the interaction is for some other member of the group to tell another story or to relate another anecdote. Of course, this second story cannot be *any* story: in highly complex ways the second narration has to share certain informational and thematic features with the first story, and generally speaking, and up to a certain point, the more it has in common with the preceding story the more the conversational group will accept it as a natural and appropriate new long turn in the conversation. Further, the second story will be expected to extend some aspect of the first story — in the classic instance it will attempt to 'cap the previous anecdote'.

If we now take this attested conversational phenomenon and attempt to apply it metaphorically to the writing of Article-Introductions, something like the following interpretation will emerge. The researcher completes his research, writes up his results or has them in the form of substantial notes. This is the second story. He then considers his introduction — there is some evidence that introductions, although appearing *first* on paper, are often written *late* (Dudley-Evans, personal communication). His introduction will be, amongst other things, his version of the relevant previous research to be written as a 'first story' so that his original 'second story' can extend or 'cap' it. Now in order to achieve a successful second story (in order to obtain a round of academic applause), our researcher has to proceed with certain care. For one thing, he needs to establish that the composite first story is 'cappable' by his own story; therefore he needs to ensure that his second story is preceded by remarks and hints that demonstrate that the composite first story of previous research is not a complete or completely successful one. Equally importantly, he needs to show something else. He needs to establish early on that all the stories are *serious* and *non-trivial* — that the combined story is relevant to wider issues whatever superficial indications there may be to the contrary. It also follows, of course, that the weaker the second story, the more careful must be the first story preparation for it.

4. Applications to the Teaching of Academic Writing

The third and final conclusion I would like to draw relates closely to the theme of this volume. I have already made reference to Project Writing courses for overseas students, and to hopes that an investigation into Article-Introductions would improve my teaching materials in this area. It has happened that over the last two years I have also become involved with Communication Skills courses for British postgraduate students, largely in connection with Aston's Interdisciplinary Higher Degrees Scheme. To my relief (and some surprise) many of my ESP-type activities seem to be quite well received by native speakers, the only substantial modification I have made being, as might be expected, a fairly severe pruning of the more mechanical and code-related language activities. I now summarize some of the activities that I have found suitable for both overseas and native-English postgraduate students.

(1) *Colour-Coding*
Sets of marker-pens (4 different colours) are used for marking up the structure of Article-Introductions. The 4-part structure I presented

earlier operates as a 'template' against which my examples, or instances contributed by the class, can be measured. Typically, three types of result emerge:

(a) The introduction fits.

(b) The introduction fits, but one of the four moves is missing.

(c) The introduction does not fit.

(2) *Finding a Metaphor*

The aim here is to try and gain agreement about 'the plot within the plot'.

(a) Is the introduction best seen as a *problem-solution* text-type or a *second-story*?

(b) In either case, to what extent is it a *'straw-man'* argument?

(c) To what extent is the summary of previous research an *ego-trip* for the author or authors?

(3) *Referencing*

I ask the students to analyse and reflect upon their own writing-up of previous research. Which of the three options do they tend to use — central reporting, parenthetical reporting or non-reporting? Then follow discussion and exercise work on stylistic variation and its implications, exercises on placing parenthetical references after noun phrases or at the end of sentences, and consideration of the advantages and disadvantages of each.

(4) *Jumbled Introductions*

These are re-assembly exercises, initially with the MOVES out of order, subsequently with the individual sentences (on separate slips of paper) in random order.

(5) *Writing up Scholarly Introductions*

The class is presented with a number of simulated library research cards containing the main findings from about ten pieces of published research, and the title and abstract of each article, the introduction for which is about to be written. The library research cards are so constructed that at least one can be dismissed as being irrelevant, and the remainder present interesting questions regarding the merits of chronological, thematic or 'for-and-against' ordering.

My groups of students report that they find the analytic work in (1) to (4) makes them more critical and more perceptive readers of both their own work and of articles in journals. The most interesting aspect of the feedback from the more creative activities such as (5) is that usually we all agree that there seem to be several quite different but equally acceptable ways of assembling and framing a particular selection of previous research material, and that the way which we choose as particular individuals is probably more a reflection of our own cognitive predispositions than of some cognitive structure inherent in the content.

5. Postscript

The possible ways of structuring the Introduction itself seem not to be explicitly recognized by the sections of the community that read and write such scholarly articles. I have over the last year or so given seminars on Article-Introductions to various groups of M.A. students of Applied Linguistics/EFL, and usually with a certain number of lecturing staff also in attendance. I begin by asking participants to put the following 7 sentences plus title into the original order.

(1) Nevertheless more experimental data are required and in particular it would seem desirable to make experiments on glassy samples whose properties can be varied slightly from one to the other.

(2) The thermal conductivity has a plateau which is usually in the range 5 to 10K and below this temperature it has a temperature dependence which varies approximately as T^2.

(3) Some progress has been made towards understanding the thermal behaviour by assuming that there is a cut-off in the photon spectrum at high frequencies (Zaitlin and Anderson, 1975a, b) and that there is an additional system of low-lying two-level states (Anderson et al., 1972; Phillips, 1972).

(4) The specific heat below 4K is much larger than that which would be expected from the Debye theory and it often has an additional term which is proportional to T.

(5) The present investigation reports attempts to do this by using various samples of the same epoxy resin which have been subjected to different curing cycles.

(6) The thermal properties of glassy materials at low temperatures are still not completely understood.

(7) THE THERMAL CONDUCTIVITY AND SPECIFIC HEAT OF EPOXY RESIN FROM 0.1 TO 80K.

(8) Measurements of the specific heat (or the diffusivity) and the thermal conductivity have been taken in the temperature range 0.1 to 80K for a set of specimens which covered up to nine different curing cycles.

(Kelham and Rosenburg, 1981)

I estimate that between 60–70 pairs of people have tried this exercise, but to date not one pair has succeeded in arranging the seven sentences into their original sequence of: 7-6-2-4-3-1-5-8. Why should this be? Given the composition of the groups, failure can hardly be ascribed to weaknesses in the English language or to some intellectual deficiency; nor has anybody suggested that the introduction itself is not a proper text or deals with a subject matter so technical that some 'general understanding' of the argument is impossible. The most likely explanation, therefore, for the unexpected difficulty of the task is that those attempting the exercise could not call upon any useful expectations as to how the Introduction might be arranged (as they doubtless could in more explicitly understood genres such as *Laboratory Reports* or *Business Letters*). In fact, this explanation has been supported by the fact that when the members of the seminar groups have been asked to have another go after hearing my description of the most common 'generalized plot' in Article-Introductions, the success rate has usually climbed from 0% to about 50%.

Notes

1. I would like to thank Vijay Bhatia for his research assistance.
2. The choices available at MOVE TWO are more complex than at the other moves and so have not been listed here. They are discussed in *Aspects of Article-Introductions* (Swales, 1981), cited in the References.

References

DUDLEY-EVANS, TONY 'A Communicative Approach to the Teaching of Writing', in Richards, D. (ed.) *Communicative Course Design, RELC* Occasional Papers No. 17, Regional English Language Centre: Singapore, 1981.
HILL, JANE H. and HILL, KENNETH C. 'Honorific Usage in Modern Nahuatl', *Language*, **54**, 1, 1978.
JORDAN, R. R. *Academic Writing Course*, Glasgow: Collins, 1980.
KELHAM, S. and ROSENBURG, H. H. 'The Thermal Conductivity and Specific Heat of epoxy resin from 0.1 to 80K', in *J.Phys.C.: Solid State Physics*, **14**, 1981.
O'CONNOR, MAEVE and WOODFORD, PETER F., *Writing Scientific Papers in English*, Amsterdam: Elsevier, 1976.
SWALES, JOHN, *Aspects of Article Introductions*, Language Studies Unit, University of Aston in Birmingham, 1981.

Editor's Comment

John Swales' thoughtful and incisive investigation into the structure of Article-Introductions is clearly of relevance to both L1 Communication Studies and L2 ESP—both for students and specialist academic staff. Swales has focussed on the applications of his research to teaching academic writing. But an understanding of the structure of Article-Introductions is equally relevant in an academic *reading* course, in that it offers a predictable structure against which the reader can 'mesh' the specific content of the Introduction, and thus it allows easier processing of what is often rather difficult reading matter.

RCW

NEWCASTLE POLYTECHNIC'S WRITING CENTRE AND ITS ORIGINS: A DESCRIPTION OF AN INNOVATION

CHRIS DE WINTER HEBRON

Newcastle Polytechnic

Introduction

This article describes a development in the teaching of writing skills at undergraduate level – the Newcastle Polytechnic Writing Centre – which is, apparently, unique at the moment in British higher education (Heywood, 1980). In America, however, where the Writing Centre concept started, it is by no means unique, and it was there that I first encountered it.

1. The North American Problem

The basic problem which the American Writing Centre movement addressed grew out of the mass nature of American college education. As enrolments increased and as more groups within the population came to attend college, it became increasingly obvious that the sophisticated elaborate speech and writing skills that instructors traditionally expected from students were just not being acquired by many freshmen. Responses to the 'events of 1968' – affirmative action, open colleges and the like – all simply brought in more and more and more students who just *could not write*.

One possibility might have been to declare them under-qualified and to throw them off the course; but even if this had been ideologically acceptable at the time, the numbers involved were too large, and anyway some sort of legal, maybe even moral commitment had been made.

So remedial courses were instituted – courses known colloquially as 'Bonehead English'. They did not work terribly well: bored, contemptuous teachers were teaching – or rather failing to teach – bored, contemptuous students what the system said they had to learn, but said in tones which suggested it did not mean it.

2. Moves Towards a Solution

One of the earliest attempts to suggest something better – and to my mind, one of the best – came in an article written by Roger Garrison, roughly six years later, in 1974, called 'One to One: Tutorial Instruction'. Here is how it begins:

"Twenty-five years of frustration with the usual methods of teaching freshman composition were quite enough. I was fed up, as most English teachers are, with endless stacks of mediocre papers piling up relentlessly every week, every month, all year; with minimum student improvement, despite my efforts; and with the increasingly defeated sense that a slob culture's effect on student language habits was much too strong for a mere school effort to combat.

I had been a professional writer before I became a school-teacher. I knew that school, even a fine liberal arts college and graduate study on top of that, hadn't taught me to write. (Indeed, graduate school had a negative influence.) So, when I had an opportunity at a small college, with perfectly ordinary, pleasant, unmotivated students, I determined to try to teach them how to write in much the same ways that I had finally learned — in ways that most professionals learn: by self-instruction, with the guidance and help of an editor. . . .

Traditional methods of freshman composition instruction are teacher-oriented and text-oriented, and are grossly inefficient. (If the writing of the typical college graduate is any measure, the methods are also ineffective.) The teacher designs the assignments, guides the reading, conducts the class, grades the papers; and, if he is conscientious, laboriously handwrites comments, admonitions, and instructions on returned papers. Typically, class time is spent talking about readings assigned as examples of good writing; talking about forms and styles and devices of writing; or discussing good points and bad points of student papers. All the while the talking is going on, the students are not learning how to write.

Students may be learning (a) how others have written, (b) what techniques have (apparently) been used by professionals to achieve certain effects, (c) what grammatical errors to avoid, (d) how to respond to the questions at the end of each segment of a 'College Reader', and (e) not least, how to write for the demands, quirks, prejudices, and tastes of a particular instructor (how to pass the course). But busy as all this may keep a freshman it will be largely irrelevant to the business of learning to write.

The plain fact is that writing is learned while writing — and re-writing — and in no other way. All professional writers know this."

That struck a chord in me when I read it: maybe it will in you too. A little later on, he has this to say in elaboration of that final 'plain fact' (p. 58):

"Assumptions about teaching writing — mostly sound and defensible: *Premise*: To teach others to learn to write you need to know — clearly and in detail — what the act of writing is and how a writer works. *Premise*:   A writer is any person who successfully communicates thoughts, information, ideas, feelings or any material from experience, in writing to others.

The following assumptions complement the foregoing premises.
— Writing is a craft, a skill which can be acquired through diligent and systematic practice. (Writing can also be an art. But almost any craft can become an art: it depends on the genius of the craftsman. Craftsmanship comes first.)
— There is no right or wrong in writing. There is only what communicates and what does not communicate.
— A group (a class) has no writing problems; there are only individuals who have problems saying what they mean.
— A writing teacher is a good listener, a fast reader, a good diagnostician: in short, an editor-on-the-spot.
— The major training device in learning how to write is *re-writing*.
— The attempt to write often generates much of what you want to say."

Garrison also attacks the use of conventional class meetings for teaching writing in these terms:

> "A Class of twenty-five to thirty-five students and a teacher make up An Administrative Convenience. Their very organization and scheduling require that they have group meetings and involve themselves in group efforts. This means a lot of talking. Writing is not learned by talking about it. Writing is not learned by talking about essays read for 'homework' and by responding to questions about the essays. Writing is not learned by discussing forms and techniques. The student learns writing when he is writing. Period."

That struck a chord in me, too, and apparently also in quite a number of Roger Garrison's North American readers.

Despite his dislike of 'Administrative Conveniences', Garrison's own paper described how such a concept could be put into practice within a conventional composition — we would probably say 'Communication' — class. Within a few months, however, such colleges as Golden West College, California were abandoning the conventional scheduled class approach in favour of a Writing Centre (I believe they may have coined the term) — a single physical location to which students could come, and where they could work in groups or on their own, with a tutor or independently, in 'courses' that were structured to individual study, that were of varying lengths and levels, and that could interlock to form an entire Freshman Composition course if required, or could simply deal with a specific student problem (Golden West 1976). Professor Ann Hostetler, who runs the Centre today, tells me however that they still have the problems of *having* to register a minimum number of students for a specific 'course' before it can be run even though the students may be studying individually: The 'Administrative Convenience' clearly dies hard.

3. The Competency-Based Approach

A second approach to the problem developed from the notion of competency-based learning. University of Waterloo (Ontario)'s 'English Language Proficiency Programme', started in 1976, will do well as an example. As a response to the 'bonehead invasion', it works, so to speak, by defining how bony a *soft* head may legitimately be: it gives all freshmen a proficiency test in English writing which is both qualifying and diagnostic.

Students 'failing' it (who have to 'pass' eventually to take their degree) are assigned to the Waterloo Writing Clinic where they work *individually* with tutors. The size of the problem at Waterloo can be judged from the following paragraph from a letter to me written on 29th October, 1980 by Alan McLachlin, the Clinic's current Supervisor:

> "As (our) newsletter may have made apparent — I have not seen it — our arrangements here are comparable (to yours) in some ways, but it would appear, both more extensive and less varied. That is, we have a Writing Clinic, staffed by 24 part-time tutors, presently offering

one-to-one tutorial assistance to some 360 students per week. But we are dealing, in general, with minimal competence in writing; . . . And the students in our Clinic are, at least this year, only rarely self-referred; some are recommended by their professors as needing help; most — 95% — failed the English Language Proficiency Examination which freshmen must write on first coming to the University of Waterloo".

Notice the linking of the words 'Clinic', 'failed', 'needing help' and 'minimal competence' in that statement, by the way. The careful examination of what students need, and the individual tuition, I like; but the whole pseudo-medical metaphor used for thinking about it gives me the shudders — I somehow feel they are going to start vivisecting the students any minute, though the rational part of my mind knows perfectly well that Alan McLachlin is a sincere and immensely hardworking man who cares deeply about students with writing and reading problems. Perhaps it is this way of thinking which is the biggest single disadvantage of the whole competency-based approach.

4. The 'Trouble-Shooting' Approach

Finally, in order of development — though I actually came across it first — University of Maryland University College in 1978 started a walk-in and appointment individualized 'trouble-shooting' service for students (or indeed anyone) interested in writing better. UMUC, as it is colloquially known, is a remarkable institution; it deals *entirely* with part-time and distance-learning students (probably the largest number of any college in the world), has campuses spread all over the state, holds classes in police stations, and even has offshoots in England, Germany, and Japan, for working with students serving in the American forces. Because of its unusual student groups, it has had to develop flexible and innovative methods, and indeed now houses the Secretariat of IUT — the International Conference on Improving University and College Teaching. The Centre's main activities are described in an article by Mary Anna Dunn, its first Tutor, in *Faculty Forum*, the UMUC Staff journal, and are further elaborated in the following letter of 27th September, 1978:

"Primarily, I work with individuals on whatever writing they are doing at the time, whether it be a research paper, a report, or a job application letter. For those who want general help on skills, I ask them to prepare a writing sample and often give a diagnostic test that covers sentence structure, grammatical agreement, and punctuation. Each session evolves according to the client's needs. Most sessions are approximately thirty minutes long, and clients often return more than once. So far, clients have ranged from pre-enrollees to faculty members, with all levels in between.

"We are spreading the word about the Writing Center in various ways, all of which have brought in some clients. My presence at registration seemed to help too. The enclosed hand-out is available in the lobby of the Center of Adult Education and from academic advisors. A poster in the Center has led a few people here, and periodic announcements are published in the monthly student newsletter. I encourage other instructors to tell their students about the Writing Center and do so myself at every opportunity. As for faculty, the Forum article is our main contact, and I have made announcements at faculty orientation meetings and in informal personal contacts. I hope that the referral slip (printed in the Forum) will alert both faculty and students to the service as well as provide a small degree of coercion to bring students in.

"Informing our various office staffs has been important also, since people may not know the right number to call and may need to be referred appropriately. Many students seem to feel more comfortable about coming in if they have spoken with me by telephone first. The arrangement whereby I call inquirers back has worked well. (This pattern is necessary since I do not have daytime office hours.) Some inquiries can be handled entirely by telephone.

"I nearly forgot to mention that I supplement the tutorial sessions with hand-outs on transitions, connectives, etc., and that we do have a few books to loan with exercises on vocabulary, verb usage, study techniques and other relevant topics. Also, on the College Park campus is the Reading and Study Skills Laboratory, where students can go for additional help. The RSSL has a wide assortment of books and study tapes on all sorts of topics. Our approach is tutorial; theirs, self-study. (That their hours are not convenient for UMUC students was a major reason for establishing our own Writing Center).

"Some of the logistics of our operation are unusual in that our students are all part-time and all commuters. Most have full-time jobs during the day. In a situation where students live on Campus, a tutorial centre is probably easier to establish, in that they can drop in more conveniently. Nevertheless, I have been pleased with the response so far this fall. The students who come are surely motivated, since they must either make a special trip or come to campus early before their classes."

All these approaches are based on a number of common premises, it seems to me. Put briefly, they are:
   (a) You can teach people *about* writing, but you cannot, in the end, teach them *how* to write. You can only *help them learn*.
   (b) People will only learn to write *if they want to*.
   (c) Everybody's writing problems or interests are different (though, to be sure, there is enough common ground for some group work to take place).

5.   The Problem in Britain

Britain, of course (we smugly say) has not the 'bonehead English' — sorry, 'minimal competence' — problem that has plagued North America, partly because our education system is more elitist and therefore requires more from the intending student in the way of qualifications and skills, and partly because most of our more specialist undergraduate courses never actually demand a formal measurement of students' ability to write. We may say this, but we are wrong on both counts. In the first place, the growth of multiple-choice examinations means that there is increasingly less need for the qualifications and skills demanded by a conventional two A-level entry to include ability to write a coherent undergraduate-style essay (still less a project report). In the second place, it is certainly not uncommon for tutors to reduce the grade or mark of an under-graduate essay for lack of order, or structure, or organized presentation — all *writing* skills — or even in some cases plain old-fashioned 'grammar' (by which the tutor usually, in my experience, means 'syntax', but I will not belabour the point). And, of course, three groups of British institutions — the Technological Universities, the Polytechnics, and the Colleges of Higher Education — do actually put on formal courses in this area, through their 'Communication' or 'General Studies' programmes.

I have worked almost all my academic life in institutions from these three groups. Like Roger Garrison, I had experienced conventional 'Communication' classes for many years, at every level from pre-apprenticeship to post-graduate. Like him, I had found that they did not work — or, to be precise, did not work *well enough*. In *almost every* class there were *some* students who wanted to and did learn, but a lot of others who did not: *in some* classes, particularly those specially put on at the request of individual firms, *almost every* student wanted to learn, but often to learn something different from the others. For years, my colleagues had been saying, 'if only we could work with the students who *want* to learn, *when* they want to learn'! Spurred on by the letter from Mary Anna Dunn quoted above, I began in September 1979 to design and operate the Newcastle Centre, with the help of a range of colleagues in the School of English and History.

6. The Newcastle Centre

The Centre's physical location is in a room on the ground floor of the Polytechnic's Lipman Building, located between the student cafeteria and the senior common room, with access from each. The general plan is as shown in Figure 1.

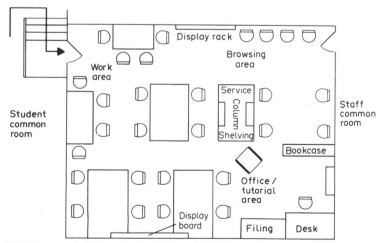

Figure 1. *The Newcastle Polytechnic Writing Centre*

The room, approximately 7m × 5.5m, is divided by an offset shelving and service column into three areas — an office/tutorial area, a browsing area, and a work area for up to 20 students. The room is windowless, except for lights over the tops of each door, and shielded fluorescent lighting is fitted, capable of being varied to provide illumination to the office, display rack and display board areas, to the browsing and work areas, or to the whole room evenly.

The choice of premises is deliberate: it used to be the sick room, and I had to fight the Health and Safety people quite hard to get it — and then the faculty administration equally hard to prevent classes being timetabled into it. It is unlocked whenever the building is open, and normally one set of the lights burns continuously to invite people in (we use up a fair number of fluorescent tubes). Its position next to the student common room means students can come in and out during free time without showing themselves up before staff: it also means they can readily slip out for, or bring in, coffee and light refreshments when using the room during a coffee or lunch break. Its location also means that students do not have far to go to reach it, even if they are not normal users of the Lipman common room: the centre is less than five minutes' walk from the Library, the Student's Union, and the campus halls of residence. Similarly, its other communicating door to the staff common room means staff can come in to see clients without making it obvious to other students. It is not a classroom: the posters on the walls and the armchair layout, I hope make that clear (though one piece of equipment I could actually still do with is a washable surface I could use as a 'white board' to demonstrate things to people — particularly note-making skills). It thus fulfils most of Bradford's (1979) requirements for a 'study centre'.

So if it is not classroom, what is it then? Well, basically, it is a resource room. We have books on writing skills: we have files of handouts on the central column, designed for independent student use. The publicity material for the centre, sent out at regular intervals, lists very clearly the range of things that we do:

(1) Browsing — students can simply come in and look around, pick up books, read bits of them, go through file boxes and remove any material they think will be helpful (a fair part of the Centre's budget is reprographic replacement).

(2) Independent study, using print materials: the handouts, typically, consist of some student hints and instructions, followed by some exercises. Often all the students need is practice in *doing* the exercises: if they want formal correction (not many in fact do) they can put their work in a wallet pinned on the display board, and I guarantee a return to them through the college mail service within 48 hours. (Keeping these guarantees is, I believe, crucially important).

(3) Tutorial guidance, study planning, trouble shooting: students, typically, come to me with "I've got this problem . . .". They contact me in one of three ways — they just walk in (some very persistent ones actually seek me out in my personal room on the 3rd floor while I have escaped for lunch or coffee!), they phone me up, or they fill in a brief

form, kept in a wallet on the outside of the door to the students' common room, outlining their problem and saying when they are free. I guarantee a return form, booking them an appointment, within 24 hours. (Again, keeping these guarantees is crucially important.) Maybe they just come and talk once. Maybe they come back a few times. Some come intermittently, just to discuss a piece of writing — a lab report, say — whenever they have one due. Some come every week for a term or even a year.

(4) Structured individualized learning programmes, using the Centre's materials, working one student (occasionally two) to one tutor at a set hour every week: this is where the help of my colleagues mostly comes in.

(5) And finally, for those students who have specific problems in common, there are brief (3-7 week) 'mini-courses' on particular writing and study skills: these often have specific links with books available in the 'browsing service', for follow-up.

I also do a little preliminary investigation for students with suspected dyslexia (running at present at one a fortnight) before putting them in touch with the North-East Dyslexia Association, and have authored with Pat Swift (our Student Union Welfare Officer) a set of notes for guiding tutors faced with such dyslexic students.

How do students learn about us? Here, my main break with tradition has been to go direct to the students themselves. Copies of our publicity leaflets are distributed to freshers on arrival, by the Students' Union: further copy is printed in the souvenir issue of *Trident* (the student newspaper) at the beginning of each year. Copies of our various announcements throughout the year go direct to student departmental notice boards throughout the institution. The mini-courses, however, *are* also advertised to Directors of Studies ('Course Leaders') as they concern specific writing skills that relate to student coursework assignments. At present — though it is difficult to be precise — about two students come to us off their own bat for each one referred by their course tutor. We also advertise through Student Services.

What sort of problems do we get? The list on Page 2 of this year's September leaflet *Help With Writing* indicates the sort of variety involved:
— Improving spelling
— Writing grammatical sentences
— Saying precisely what you mean in a lab. report
— Coherent paragraphing
— Reading for essays
— Planning specific essays in Creative Arts
— Coping with a 'writing block' ('I sit down and I just can't write!')
— Drafting a 'Science & Society' continuity essay

— Writing an appropriate letter of application for a placement post in quantity surveying
— Working out what the 'rubrics' in physics exam questions actually tell you to do
— Working to an exam-style deadline
— Coping with cross-laterality (a mild neurological problem).

And of course, there is always overlap with the study skills and writing mini-course material, for students who for some reason could not attend those meetings. And perhaps, too, I might add two particularly interesting problems new this year—one, an overseas student who can write English quite well, for ordinary purposes, but can think at an abstract level only in Farsi, and the other a student who because of his background *speaks* perfect English (as a birth tongue), but has through all his school education *written* in Arabic script. All in all, we spent 155 hours on writing skills with a total of 42 students during the 1980 Autumn term, plus a further 160 hours with another 38 students on study skills, during the first five weeks of that term, and during the first two months of the 1981 Spring term have clocked up another 168 hours with 37 more students. Students have come from six of our eight Faculties—the exceptions being Education (located on a different campus) and Management.

7. Where do we go from here?

Future developments in the Centre's work, at the moment, seem likely to be four: first, and simplest, is an extension of the 'mini courses'. Several course designs have been acquired from American centres (primarily Golden West), and the materials for them are now also in stock. We hope during the summer to be able to revise some of these for British use on a trial basis next year. The second development is a computer-managed interactive tutorial system for remedial work on spelling and grammatical sentence construction. This should have been on-stream this term, available from terminals in all buildings on the City campus at any time to any student signing on with a special user number. The programmes, from Notre Dame University, were substantially rewritten to bring them in line with British usage during last Summer and Autumn. Unfortunately we have had technical problems with the HARRIS system on which they are being implemented, but the service should be available later this year (with luck!). Third—a departure from 'writing' in the strict sense—is the development of material on the presentation of papers. This is in response to growing student demand: a first seminar for Librarianship students on the presentation of conference papers was held in February 1981, and we are negotiating with Law students over the provision of video-self-confrontation sessions for advocacy skills. Our fourth area of development involves not new work but an extension of our services. We had our first *part-time* student in the Autumn term of 1980—a Surveyor. I would like to extend our provision to all part-time courses (including evening-only), and indeed to outside clients from the City on payment of a fee, on an analogous basis to the *Telelang* system for learning languages, operated by the Polytechnic's School of Modern Languages. The demand is certainly there: we have actually had to turn away business from a leading firm of Estate Agents. But the administrative problems are complex, as Maryland found out when they started their Centre.

8. The English Studies Connection

To end this paper, let me just touch briefly on how the Centre's work relates to more conventional language teaching. First, the relationship with Communication classes: ideally, I think, most Communication teachers would like it immensely if all their work on writing problems could be conducted in this way. Certainly there is no feeling that the two conflict. Communication teachers in fact refer their students with specific writing problems to the Centre like any others. (I try my best *not* to allocate them back to their Communication teacher as a tutor, where the possibility exists!) This enables Communication classes to concentrate on a more analytical study of the communication process, and on formal discipline-related material (for example, style guides for Chemists, specific report requirements for Building Service Engineers, and so on). Indeed, I teach two such courses myself — one for Medical Laboratory Scientific Officers (which includes discussion of private languages, computer pathology testing and diagnosis, and hospital applications of word processing), and one for HND Building (which includes analysis of the construction of The Royal Institute of Chartered Surveyors' reports).

Similarly, we carefully divide off the Centre's work from our formal EFL provision for overseas students: in fact, I not infrequently refer such students who come to me straight to my colleague who runs the EFL service. Where a student's problems are located directly in *written* English however, or where — like my Farsi thinker — they are special in kind, we do take them on board. (Experimentally, I am working with the Farsi thinker on the last book of the British Council/Colombia Series *Reading and Thinking in English*).

Finally, you may be surprised to learn that we include Study and Examination Skills work, mainly on the Graham Gibbs/Desmond Rutherford models. Partly, that is historical: I was doing this in fact *before* I started the Writing Centre, and just carried on. But also we believe that these skills, almost all of which include organising information or using language, and several of which *do* involve writing, belong logically with a writing skills service. They complete the service; and in so doing, they set 'learning to write' in a context not of 'English' with all its school subject overtones, but of 'learning to be an independent student'. And that context, it seems, is one that the students themselves find acceptable.

References

BRADFORD, M. "Study Centres", *Teaching at a Distance*, **16**, Winter 1979.
DUNN, MARY ANNA "The Same Old Dragon", *Faculty Forum* (University of Maryland University College) Vol. 4. No. 4 August/September 1978.
GARRISON, R. W. "One-to-one Tutorial Instruction in Freshman Composition", *New Directions for Community Colleges*, **II**, 1, Spring 1974.
GOLDEN WEST COLLEGE *The Golden West College Writing Center Visitors' Packet*, 1976.
HEYWOOD, JOHN *Curricula, Teaching and Assessment*, address to SRHE Annual Conference, University of Surrey, December 1980.
MANN, MAUREEN *The English Language Proficiency Programme*: General Information, University of Waterloo, 1980.
MOORE, JOHN and WIDDOWSON, H. G. *Reading and Thinking in English: Discourse in Action*, Oxford: OUP, 1980.
RUTHERFORD, D. "Helping Students to Prepare for Examinations", *Teaching News*, **9**, February 1980.

Appendix

The paper you have just read is based on a demonstration of the Writing Centre I gave to a curriculum study group in 1981. Since then, I have been on a year's sabbatical leave, and the Centre has been running for that year on a reduced service ('the cuts!'). However, despite that reduction, two or three interesting developments, not all foreseen in my original paper, have in fact occurred:

(1) The computer-managed tutorial service has at last gone into operation, though still in a partly-Americanised form.

(2) A concept of 'client-groups' has been developed — students of a particular discipline or level, for whom specific mini-courses or tutorial meetings can be developed. This has also included, for the first time, students outside the Polytechnic, as predicted in the closing pages of the paper, with the development of two special mini-course series for Third World MPhil students in the Department of Architecture at Newcastle University.

(3) Plans are also now underway to develop a *cooperative* service to particular client groups, where the Centre staff will act as consultants to 'regular' course lecturers in other disciplines, jointly with their designing and teaching official elements of the students' main courses. The first of these, with a part-time BSc Hons Health Studies course, scheduled to start the day before this Conference, uses ideas borrowed from Action Learning Theory to make possible shared staff-student course design of a part of the programme called 'Study Skills and Private Study'.

A request has been made to the Nuffield Foundation for funds to develop the 'client-group' concept further: as I write this, it is too early to say whether it will be successful.

Editor's Comment

In the UK, few institutions have experimented with Writing Centres. Possibly, they have felt that assessment of communication skills was an essential component in the measure of attainment for a degree or other qualification, and therefore that a uniform programme of teaching and testing should be provided (indeed, be obligatory) for *all* students in a group. Chris Hebron's paper is valuable in showing not only that a Writing Centre can be organised successfully, but also that such a Centre need not be seen as an *alternative* to a formal CS programme.

He also emphasises that people learn to write only *if they want to*. He thus has much in common with the approaches described in this volume by Brigid Ballard and Kenneth James. Unfortunately, the conference did not discuss in detail how to overcome the lack of motivation that many teachers find in their students, even in overseas students who need help to acquire enough English to cope with their special-subject classes. This seems to us an important topic for research at the earliest opportunity.

JK

THE WRITING OF THESES BY SPEAKERS OF ENGLISH AS A FOREIGN LANGUAGE: THE RESULTS OF A CASE STUDY

KENNETH JAMES

University of Manchester

Introduction

For the past ten years, an important part of my work as Senior Tutor to Overseas Students has been to help post-graduate students with their written English. This assistance has been rendered in three forms: firstly, through the teaching of basic academic English as part of our intensive pre-sessional course; secondly, through the development of subject-specific English in weekly classes held during the first term; and thirdly, through the analysis and correction of short samples from the student's own essays or research-writing in the second (and final) academic term of my teaching year. This case study then, which deals with the English language supervision of a full PhD thesis, may in fact be seen as an extension of the latter work.

The student I selected for supervision, a Brazilian whom we shall call Marcos, was about to write up a piece of research in the sociology of medicine entitled 'The Structure of Health and Illness in Iguape'. A subject in the social sciences was preferred to one in the pure or applied sciences, as I judged that it would make greater demands on a student's power of self-expression, the language of many pieces of research in the physical sciences having proved in my experience to be somewhat predictable, on occasions even formulaic.

A persistent difficulty in attempting a supervision of this type is to know who should be responsible for what and when. There are times when a language supervisor ought to dictate; other times when he should defer; yet others when he would be best advised to compromise. The trade-off between the linguistic expertise of the supervisor and the special subject knowledge of the student is neither simple nor invariable. It became peculiarly difficult to manage when Marcos was himself struggling to interpret, and select from, the information he had gathered i.e. when in the student's own words his "writing very much took second place to (his) thinking".

As the thesis progressed and as each chapter moved through its various drafts, so the nature and incidence of the language mistakes requiring urgent attention was to change. In the following section of this paper, I have tried to identify three categories of such mistakes. This has been done on a scale of communicative damage. As the greatest damage occurred when Marcos was least experienced and most under pressure i.e. in the earlier months, this analysis parallels the history of the major teaching and learning events. The remainder of this paper then performs two simultaneous functions: it gives an account of the case study, while at the same time systematically analysing and discussing its results.

Analysis of Mistakes

1. Mistakes which Frequently Led to a Breakdown in Meaning

1.1 Over-long/over-complex Sentences

A non-subject specialist, I quickly learned, is far more dependent on simple English, clearly expressed, than the subject supervisor — who seemed often to use his specialized knowledge to forestall ambiguity and to tolerate complexity. (I was often amazed in fact at what the subject specialist allowed to 'pass' in this respect, and frequently found myself asking whether I was not perhaps becoming too exigent.) One type of mistake, above all others, proved damaging in the early stages: and that was when Marcos produced sentences which were over-long, and/or intricately subordinated. An example will serve to make this clear:

> "This element arrangement of these elements so classified in an antithetic bricolage from what Levi-Strauss (1970) denominated "science of the concrete" or a science which, when deprived of a well-defined basis, principles and methods by the simple fact of placing elements into a structure and transforming what would be otherwise looked as chaos into ordained arrangements, presents an intrinsic efficacy". (i)

To arrive at an acceptable version of this extract cost twenty minutes or so of hard linguistic labour. After three succeeding interpretations as to the meaning of the sentence had proved to be incorrect, I invited Marcos to reformulate what he had written. The original printed version, however, seemed to exercise a hypnotic effect on him, and so my request simply resulted (as so often in such cases) in a weak paraphrase that held stubbornly to the structure of the original. Only when the manuscript had been put to one side and when we began to discuss what he really *meant* did progress prove possible. The simpler rhythms of speech, together with the access to detailed immediate feedback, I was to find, often gave improved results. In this case, they certainly enabled us to hammer out a following improved version:

> "According to Levi-Strauss' definition, such a system of classification may be regarded as 'a science of the concrete', in that it lacks a well-defined basis, principles and methods. Even so it has an intrinsic efficacy in so far as it places elements within a coherent structure, bringing order where there would otherwise be chaos". (ii)

For various reasons this was later also thought to be unsatisfactory, particularly as it implied that the negative characteristics ("lacks a . . .") were sufficient to define a "science of the concrete". (The full-stop, placed after the word 'methods' at the end of the first sentence, produces this distortion. A full-stop is necessary, of course, in order to divide the original over-long sentence into two; but its placement required more careful thought than it received here.) The final version, re-written much later (in fact, just before the thesis was finally typed), became:

"Such a system of classification may be regarded as a science of the concrete. It lacks a well-defined basis, and a set of principles and methods, but it has an intrinsic efficacy in so far as it places elements within a coherent structure. In short, it brings order where there would otherwise be chaos". (iii)

As important as correcting such sentences, were my attempts to find out *why* Marcos had produced them in the first place. What seemed to have been happening—something which I had first begun to speculate on when I started marking the short *samples* of my students' research work two or three years previously—was that Marcos had thought in conceptual units which he invariably attempted to '*transcribe*' into sentences. When these units were internally simple and/or few in their constituent components, this 'transcription' worked well enough. When the conceptual unit was internally complex and contained a large number of constituent components, then transcription did not work. That is to say, it worked only in the sense that the thought was transferred to the page, without conveying its intended meaning to the reader. What seemed to be needed in such cases was an attempt to '*translate*' rather than transcribe: an attempt in other words to find the correspondence between the syntax that characterizes a particular piece of thinking and the syntax of the writing needed to convey it. Indeed, I would claim that evidence for the relative success of these two operations on a complex conceptual unit can be seen, at least in part, in version one (transcription) and version three (translation) of the extract quoted above. Marcos assured me that he had been perfectly clear in *his own mind* what he was *thinking* when he attempted his first version. It was just that the results of his transcription proved too difficult for the reader to handle. A more skilled writer, of course (perhaps a near-native speaker) working from wider and more accurate grammatical resources, might have been able to communicate through transcription first time off. The point is, though, that he would only have been able to do so by taking unnecessary communicative risks.

Translation, of course, puts more of the responsibility for communicating on to the writer, so that some of the burden of comprehending may be taken away from the reader. For it to work, though, the writer has to know *when* to translate and *how* to translate. The 'when', it seems, is often only decided by trial and error—that is to say, the writer writes, only to find on re-reading what he has produced, that some sentences do not, for reasons of length and intricacy, internally cohere. Even this ability to self-monitor may be so weak among the inexperienced that many statements, likely to prove unintelligible to the reader, are still allowed to go forward by the author into his first draft.

What the writer needs, of course, is to be able to predict which of his conceptual units will not transcribe. Such an ability, however, may not come easily. And even if the writer should come to possess it, he may not be able to call on a satisfactory translation straightaway. Many may find that in the more difficult types of prose composition there are occasions when one has *first* to complete a complex and clumsy transcription before one can tackle the (frequently) difficult and the (often) lengthy process of translation.

'How to translate', the second requirement for handling complex conceptional units, is a procedure which it is very difficult to specify with any clarity. It would, however, seem to involve at least some of the following operations:

- the construction of a *number* of sentences in order to communicate effectively one conceptual unit

- the *re-ordering* of some (or all) of the elements which go to make up the conceptual unit (i.e. the author has to write in a different sequence from the one in which he first started to think)

- the introduction into the writing of anaphoric and other cohesive devices in order to maintain the coherence of the original conceptual unit

- the cutting or (less often) the expanding of various conceptual elements which may need greater or less attention according to how the needs of the reader are judged.

None of these operations is easy to achieve in a first language, and some students whose experience of English has only been that of a foreign language find them particularly difficult to manage. One common and wholly inappropriate reaction for a student when faced for the first time with the problem of producing over-long and complex sentences, is simply to spray the offending section with full stops. Having checked that he has obeyed the rules of succeeding capitalization, the writer then moves on, happy in the belief that he has solved the reader's difficulties. It may only be after a considerable period of time that he learns to accept that the process of writing requires the 're-thinking' of his more complex conceptual units as part of the activity to translate their meaning effectively.

Learning in *Marcos'* case was to take place rapidly, a function no doubt of the frustration and delays we had experienced in the many earlier break-downs in communication. The complex, concept-transcribed sentences, which characterized the writing in his first twenty or thirty pages, became increasingly rare. The lesson — learned as it had been on the job — was well-learned, perhaps too well-learned. I say this because towards the end of the thesis the simple sentence almost became a mannerism. On occasions I was even to encourage an opposite procedure, namely the gathering together of a number of short, closely-related, single sentences into one longer sentence. Such encouragement was judged necessary *either* to relieve the monotony of Marcos' original (one simple sentence following another); *or* to reduce a sense of sprawl (chopping up the transcription of a complex conceptual unit into a number of separate sentences often increases the length required to express the original idea); *or* to illustrate better the differing degrees of importance and the closeness in the relationship among the separated sentences. Which is no more than to say that in writing all rules are relative. Judgement is all.

1.2   Faulty Referencing

The over-complex sentence, however, was not the only thing to cause a breakdown in communication. Faulty referencing produced the same results both in the earlier stages of the thesis and in the main body of the work as well. Unlike the complex sentence though, mistakes in this area rarely proved as serious. Normally it was easy to locate the *cause* of the problem, and it seldom took more than a minute or so to sort out what referred to what. An example which involves a typical EFL mistake may serve as an illustration. Marcos wrote —

> "What must be emphasised is the fact that science itself is problematic and cannot be taken as a neutral language to assess everything. Because of its cultural impregnation it[1] must be taken into consideration in any kind of sociological research which deals with it[2]".

If one takes this at face value then the two instances of *it* in the second sentence both refer to science. This produces nonsense. Clearly Marcos intended *it*[1] in the second sentence to refer to the section "the fact that science . . . assess everything" in the first. English, however, demands a different pronominal when the referent is as complex as this. *It*[1], then, should in fact be substituted by the word *this*. A quick check with Marcos confirmed my analysis was correct, and we were then able to proceed.

Other mistakes in the use of pronominals proved to be those which native speakers often make as well. References were often made to things which had been merely implied rather than explicitly stated in the text, i.e. the sort of thing that stays in the writer's mind rather than being recorded on the writer's page. Again, in attempts to avoid a clumsy noun-phrase repetition, Marcos sometimes would employ pronouns whose referents were not immediately identifiable. Eventually I had to caution him to check carefully every pronoun before letting me see his drafts. He remained vulnerable in this area, however, to the very end.

1.3   Lexical Difficulties

Another area which could cause serious difficulties in communication from the very earliest stages was the writer's choice of lexis. Three types of problem demanded immediate attention: specialized vocabulary, false cognates, and mis-spellings. The difficulty as regards vocabulary, a problem for the language supervisor rather than the writer, was that common words may be employed with a technical meaning. The word *presented* in "He *presented* the usual symptoms" caused delays, for example, while I was first dissuaded from substituting the word *showed* and then persuaded to consult a dictionary. I soon learned that it was necessary to be wary about suggesting changes if I was not to mislead the writer, who because of his familiarity with the English of his special subject, was often puzzled at the ignorance of an intelligent layman in this area.

The second difficulty, the use of false cognates, was only occasionally really troublesome. Certain of these cognates proved immediately recognisable because the word may rarely be used in English — *revindicate* and *provenient*, for example. The mistake proved more difficult to correct, however, with words such as *actually* (with an intended Portuguese-derived meaning of currently), and *eventually* (with an intended meaning of *consequently*).

The third difficulty, which many overseas students are prone to create, is the misunderstanding caused by mis-spellings. Clearly, strong contexts normally guide the reader to the word that the writer intended. But there were occasions when pronunciation interfered with spelling and caused a complete breakdown in meaning. I recall, for example, Marcos writing, "He was brought to low", and wondering at first whether the mistake might not reside in the *to*, which perhaps should have written in its adverbial form of *too* (a form mis-employed by overseas students to signify the presence of an intensifier). I reasoned therefore that the intended meaning was "He was brought very low" or "He was humbled". In fact, I later learned that it was the word *low* that had been mis-spelled. Marcos did not make a satisfactory distinction in his speech between / əʊ / as in *low* and /ɔ:/ as in *law*, employing the first of these two vowel phonemes for the pronunciation of both words. The sentence he had intended was, it transpired, "He was brought to *law*".

Marcos experienced a further lexical problem which cumulatively caused a great deal of damage: he was poorly equipped with verbs necessary to report the literature and argue a case from it. These have been grouped in rough semantic sets below:

(i)	(ii)	(iii)	(iv)
argue	prove	note	assume
contend	demonstrate	observe	take for granted
maintain	illustrate	refer to	suggest
hold	make clear	point out	put forward
believe	reveal	draw attention to	present (a case for)
state		focus on	imply
declare		emphasize	
		stress	

A lack of facility here meant that Marcos was not always able to make clear in an economical way the status he wished to accord to the views and research findings of other writers. While this problem occurred from the very first chapter, I only became more aware of it when the thesis was well advanced; for it was only then that I became sufficiently knowledgeable to be able to understand what Marcos thought about the various writers he was quoting, that I was able to recognize that what he was writing did not always square with what he was thinking. His general preference, for example, for such 'neutral' verbs as *state* and *declare* (see list (i) above) seemed often to hint at an authority to the passage quoted which he clearly did not think the author's arguments merited. *Hold* or *argue* would have certainly suggested his attitude better, and various changes of this type came to be made in the final stages of writing.

The other problem regarding lexis which I should like briefly to touch on, again concerns the fact that the writer lacked a sufficient range in a specialized area of his vocabulary. Marcos frequently needed to find an introductory phrase in order to make clear the background viewpoint to his sentence. He needed to be able to select from phrases of the following type:

Still on the subject of X, . . .   As far as X is concerned, . . .
A further point about Y, . . .   As regards Y, . . .

In the light of X, . . .
Viewed from the angle Y . . .

But he often seemed only able to produce the somewhat un-English "in the perspective of".

1.4 *Weaknesses in Signposting*

At the end of two months, Marcos had finished the first draft of his first chapter, and it was just about this time that I began to be aware of a problem that was to become more serious as the thesis developed and as the writer tackled sections which were more exploratory and wide-ranging rather than narrow and descriptive. The problem was one of signposting. Two types may be distinguished. Firstly, there is the type which gives the reader directions at the micro-level—that is to say, signposts which show the connections between sentences or groups of sentences inside the paragraph. And secondly there is the type which gives the reader directions at the macro-level—that is to say, signposts which show the relationship between large chunks of discourse and which make clear where the global argument is leading. The first type caused occasional difficulties, largely when Marcos chose not to introduce a sentence connective which might have helped me to understand a relationship more easily. Greater difficulty, though, was to occur when he showed himself unaware of the various uses of *however*. The following sentence, for example, caused a considerable delay:

"In fact, the practice of this chemist, however influenced by knowledge from University, coincides with popular beliefs in many aspects".

As originally written (in the form which it appears above) this did not fit the sense of the overall paragraph. The problem lay with the *however* which, it later transpired, should have been an *inter-sentence connective* rather than the adverbial (modifying *influenced*) that appeared here. Once this mistake had been located, the insertion of a following comma proved enough to put things right.

The second type of signposting—at the macro-level—frequently caused serious difficulties and will be discussed here in rather more detail. First, though, a rough classification. For the purposes of this particular study I found it helpful to distinguish four types: the introducer, the recapitulator, the link and the concluder. Lack of a wide experience in writing in his *first* language, particularly as regards extended pieces of some complexity, meant that even if Marcos had been employing his native language he would have had difficulty in the phrasing of such signposts. But it is not simply a case of knowing *how* to write these, nor even how to write them in English. Equally—perhaps even more important—is to be able to judge *when* to make use of such devices.

The recapitulator—

"So far in our analysis of X we have suggested that A, B and C might be significant factors"

—and the link

"Our conclusions as regards X prompt a further question in relation to Y. It is to this question that we must now turn"

were conspicuous by their absence. I thus frequently found myself asking Marcos whether such devices might not with advantage be inserted. Certainly without them I all too often lost track of the argument, or found that the movement from one section to another was jerky or even puzzling.

Again the question must be asked as to *why* Marcos found such difficulty in these areas. One reason has already been alluded to, namely, he had little experience in writing extended passages of academic prose. It is my belief, in fact, that many British tutors underestimate how much their native students are advantaged by the strong essay-based tradition of our educational system, and how far many overseas students are correspondingly disadvantaged by coming from a background where this is lacking.

But lack of first-language experience is not the only reason. Signposting of this type is rarely given much attention in writing courses for overseas students. Very few learners of English as a Foreign Language, after all, are going to write such extended pieces of prose. And even if the numbers were to increase dramatically, a potential publisher would still have problems. Realistic practice in performing such a language function would require a large number of lengthy chunks of discourse. The ratio of language exercise to number of pages is likely to be unacceptably low. And anyway, it may be that this kind of signposting is best taught on the job. This was certainly what we found in Marcos' case.

2.   Mistakes which Frequently Led to a Blurring of the Meaning

So far the mistakes I have analysed (with one single exception that will be discussed at the end) are those which tended seriously to damage communication. They all, at one time or another, interrupted my reading, and most of them required prolonged attention at the first-draft stage. The category of mistakes I shall deal with in this second section also made it difficult for me to extract a satisfactory meaning, but the difficulties here were of a different order. Whereas mistakes in the first category caused a *breakdown* in meaning, the mistakes that I shall analyse here resulted in a *blurring* of the meaning. Thus I would read a passage, the sentences of which were perfectly well-formed, only to be left with a sense of not having obtained a clear picture of the global meaning. While I was able to say what the writer was *talking about*, I found it more difficult to be certain about what he was *getting at*. It was noticeable that the type of mistake which produced this effect was most often recognized at second-draft stage, when I began to make greater demands on the writer as regards understanding his message.

2.1   Inefficient Ordering

The most clear-cut mistake in this second category proved to be 'inefficient ordering'. I found, for example, that I would settle on one aspect of a subject in a first sentence of a paragraph, then move to a second aspect in the next two sentences, only to move back to the first aspect in sentence four, finally returning to the second aspect again in the remainder of the paragraph: a journey from A to B, back to A and then back to B again. It was usually necessary to conflate separate sentences appearing at scattered points in a paragraph, by means of clause subordination or even phrase in apposition, in order to correct such faults.

2.2   Inappropriate Weighting

A second problem which produced 'blur' resulted from inappropriate weighting. This occurred, for example, when Marcos wanted to give equal importance to two points, the first of which had received an extensive treatment in the literature and the second of which had been less thoroughly treated. He tended in such a situation to produce a section which was grotesquely lop-sided. It may be objected of course that this is a content-specific problem — something to be dealt with by the writer himself or by his special-subject supervisor. While there may be some merit to this argument, the fact remains that even when Marcos himself recognized (at second-draft stage) that he had thus spent too long on one point, he often had considerable difficulty in summarizing. In other words, this was as much a matter of language competence as special subject skill.

2.3   Functional Incoherence

The third and final problem in this second category of mistakes was what I have chosen to describe as *functional incoherence*. In certain stages of Marcos' work, he had to narrate, to describe, to analyse, to argue and to discuss—all in a relatively short stretch of prose. In other words, he was engaged in producing the sort of account one often reads in a standard text-book of history. An incident is described, a reason is given, a key personality or institution is analysed, a theory is explored, etc. etc. The writer moves from one function (say, that of description) to a second (say, that of explanation) while threading the whole account on a narrative string. Unfortunately, this kind of writing is peculiarly hard to manage even for a native speaker. If it is not done with considerable skill, the sense of direction and indeed the overall aim of particular passages may become blurred. Transitions between the sentences (or sections) which perform these various functions can be difficult to handle; there also has to be a nice exercise of judgement as regards the arrangement and weighting of information. All of this brings us back to the first two types of mistake which were dealt with in this section, completing what all too often threatened to become a vicious circle.

3. Mistakes which Distracted the Reader from the Meaning Conveyed

From the point of view of communicating meaning, we have seen that two categories of mistake—those which produce *breakdowns* and those which give rise to *blur*—are significant at the first and second-draft stage. The category I shall consider in this section tended not to affect the meaning at all. That is to say, I was able to read through whole passages in which such mistakes occurred without having to stop in order to work out what the writer meant. At worst, I found myself simply distracted. So whereas the mistakes included in category 1 and category 2 had to be corrected in order that the message might be made fully and properly *comprehensible*, mistakes in the category I am about to describe received attention in order to make the message stylistically and grammatically *acceptable*.

3.1 Stylistic Acceptability

In this section I shall first explore the *reasons* why Marcos found an acceptable style difficult to achieve. I shall then go on to describe and discuss the different types of *mistake* he made.

The Reasons

● *Sociocultural.* Marcos, as he explained in great detail to me (for this was a question I took up with him on more than one occasion), had received a training in writing that was very different from that which a comparable British student might have received. An analysis of the number and length of the essays he had completed at school and university, for instance, suggested that he had had much less experience of extended writing than his British counterpart. And then the one course he had taken which had addressed itself to questions of style had encouraged him to 'complexify' what he had hitherto been content to write simply, and to render ornate what he had originally left plain. When one also considers that the bulk of what Marcos read in English came from the literature of sociology, a discipline renowned neither for its economy nor simplicity of expression, we have perhaps gone some way towards explaining the basis for some of his problems.

But there is much more to the matter than this, for the majority of the staff at the Brazilian University that Marcos attended were heavily Marxist. (This seems to be common in all Latin-American countries where there is sufficient freedom of expression to allow it.) The students, and particularly the students in the Social Science Faculty, were much more politicized than their English equivalents. The course essay came to have for them a value which was very different from that which it had for their English contemporaries. A great deal of political energy was channelled into such writing, as the students felt they had few other outlets. Many students, and Marcos numbered himself as one of these, frequently used their special subject essay to express the moral indignation and to give vent to the political outrage that they felt. Many subject specialists, according to Marcos, were tolerant of such a practice, perhaps because they recognized that this was a stage through which young people in that society would have to pass. A few even seemed to approve. All of this made it more difficult for the student to draw the line between argument and polemic when he was engaged on research at a later date in his academic career.

Marcos, in fact, abandoned his Marxism before he came to England, but for a long time after this he found it a struggle to exorcise this 'ghost in the machine'. Above all, he had to fight very hard to stop himself from making value-laden assertions, and from relating those events of which he disapproved as if they were part of some wicked conspiracy.

● *Style of the special subject.* Every discipline has a specialized language which is readily understood by practitioners, though not by the layman. The purpose of such language is not to exclude the outsider but to make communication on professional matters more precise. Unfortunately, in addition to this professional language, there occurs in much social science writing (and indeed in most specialized academic writing) a great deal of jargon. "Jargon draws not only on the vocabulary of the 'host' discipline or profession but also on the structure and style of the language to which it clings" (Duff, 1981). Sociologists frequently aim of course to make valid, precise and generalizable statements on the often imprecise data collected from observing social behaviour. In order to achieve this they are forced to adopt an 'abstract' style which guards them against misinterpretation. "The fear of being misinterpreted is in fact . . . so powerful that the writer fences in his thoughts with stout protective palissades of qualification" (Duff). But while it might be necessary to be abstract and to be circumspect on some occasions, it is not necessary to be so on all occasions. An important and a legitimate feature of a style must not be allowed to degenerate into a mannerism. Marcos, like many other writers in such specialized fields, found this injunction difficult to carry out. He often, as we shall see, found himself expressing things in a complicated and abstract manner when something simple and concrete would have served his purpose better. As English language supervisor, though, I found I had to be careful not to label professional language as jargon, *without good reason*. Thus in the phrase "the disarticulation of the old social order" Marcos resisted my attempt to substitute the vivid, more familiar *crumbling* for the more abstract and less common *disarticulation*. The latter, it transpired, had a precision for sociologists that the former lacked.

● *First language interference.* This was the problem which proved most persistent. It is often this factor which makes translation (in its conventional sense, i.e. from a foreign language) such a difficult art. A native-speaker, moreover, will not normally spend a long time (many will spend no time at all) correcting something that he understands, and as we have noted already, such errors in style rarely interfere with the meaning in any fundamental way. The overseas student, then — employing the hidden semantic biases, the lexical collocations, the favoured grammatical constructions, and the typical rhetorical devices of his own language — quickly becomes fluent in a deviant English. Such a style can be a very difficult thing to shift. The problem is, of course, exacerbated when the student employs as his native tongue a language which shares important features of grammar and lexis with English.

The Mistakes

It is now time to illustrate some typical extracts from Marcos' thesis where I judged the style to be unacceptable. I have identified five main areas in this respect and have written the alternative, which Marcos and I agreed should be substituted, *under* the original (starred) sentences.

● The first area consists of passages which were judged to be inflated or unnecessarily abstract, thus

★ ". . . they are known by the term 'caicara', which is rather derogatory a term, connoting images related to poorness and rusticity".

they are known as 'caicara', a rather derogatory term which suggests both poverty and rural backwardness.

★ ". . . I could not understand the tyranny with which the parents let themselves be submitted to by their children".

. . . I could not understand why the parents allowed their children to dominate them.

● The second area, which overlaps with the first, covers those extracts where the writer shows a preference for the complex noun phrase rather than the subordinate clause. This often robbed a sentence of the thrust that comes from employing an active verb. The sentences thus became flaccid and tedious to read.

★ ". . . The main characteristic of the transformation in the naturalistic medicine field in Iguape brought about by modern times refers to the increasing gap between the 'natural' and 'social-metaphysical' sides of the disease".

The main change that modern medicine has brought about in Iguape is to split the 'natural' and 'socio-metaphysical' sides of the disease.

● In the third area, we see a lack of balance or symmetry:

★ "From the point of view of the social structure, 'communitas' is something fluid, inconsistent, and cannot clearly be noticed".

. . . fluid, inconsistent and difficult to identify.

● The fourth area consists of examples — there are many — of verbosity.

★ "However a considerable modification of the situation has occurred as a consequence of the introduction of modern medical care to the caicara. As a consequence of this, modern official medicine has successfully competed with the traditional system of the hot and cold classification and has increasingly been gaining ground against it".

Things have changed with the introduction of modern medical care to the caicara and the old system has recently lost a lot of ground.

● And the fifth and final area covers those statements which should have been persuasive but were in fact polemical.

★ "This sociological approach to medicine in fact intends only to extend the medical field to other areas and not evaluate it critically".

This sociological approach to medicine has recently been criticized for taking the system as given, and simply extending it to other areas. The reader will be able to judge for himself in the following pages as to how far it is reasonable to evaluate it critically.

3.2 Grammatical Acceptability

Mistakes in grammar, though fairly frequent, rarely did anything more than distract. In most cases they seemed to be the result of first-language interference. They were often corrected by the writer himself when the location of the error was pointed out; they hardly ever caused any interruption to the flow of meaning. From a communicative point of view they were trivial. And therein lies a paradox, for from a language-learning point of view they revealed basic errors of performance in the grammatical code, the commission of which would normally be taken to show that the student had an unsatisfactory level of grammatical competence and by implication *language* competence. As a matter of fact, in the multiple-choice speeded grammar test we gave him, Marcos did gain a very high mark indeed, but this was of course when he was *concentrating on things grammatical.* Under the strain of composition, however, he made very frequent mistakes in subject-verb concord, the tense system, the article system, the selection of the correct relative pronoun, the selection of the correct comparative adverbial (than/that), and the correct positioning of the adverbial phrase in a sentence: all, in fact, typical problem-areas of a Portuguese speaker.

A further mistake in the verb phrase, not included in the previous list, did however cause the occasional breakdown in meaning. Marcos had a tendency to over-use parts of the modal system, particularly *may* and *might* in a way that I was eventually to find out did not reflect his intended meaning. But apart from this, all those mistakes which language teachers traditionally expend so much time and energy preventing, seemed to play a singularly small part in this overall communication of meaning. It was indeed noticeable that Marcos continued to make many of them right the way through the eighteen months or so of the supervision. Improvement only seemed to come with passages in the third and final draft when the thinking had been done to his satisfaction and he could concentrate solely on the form of the language. Certain mistakes persisted, however, though this almost seemed not to matter, for when the final draft was written and one was able to read through whole stretches of the thesis without stopping, it was not uncommon to miss these occasional mistakes altogether, and only to pick them up at the final proof-reading stage.

4. Conclusion

It would be tempting at the end of such a study to speculate what lessons one might draw from the point of view of teaching English for Academic Purposes. I shall, however, resist this temptation. For one thing, it is dangerous to generalize from one case study (though I am aware I may have been guilty of doing this in some of the analytical comments I have essayed from time to time). For another, such speculation would require a separate paper. I shall therefore confine myself to one conclusion which I would like to think might gain the support of the reader. It is this: students need help with what they find most difficult. What they find most difficult can only be discovered by observing them at work on the job.

This is the justification for this sort of case study. Perhaps more of such work ought to be done.

Reference

DUFF, A. *The Third Language*, Oxford: Pergamon, 1981.

Editor's Comment

James, in this fascinating case-study, produces a most intriguing categorization of both communicative *breakdowns* and communicative *blurs*, and also offers numerous perceptive comments as to their causes. This part of his comprehensive paper provides a large number of leads for both ESP practitioners and for those involved with native speakers of English. The extensive involvement with 'Marcos' provides a useful complement to the more generalized but roughly comparable work of Ballard. And the final conclusion is of relevance to all of us — "Students need help with what they find most difficult. What they find most difficult can only be discovered by observing them at work on the job."

JMS

IV. Experiments in Collaborative Teaching

TEACHING COMMUNICATION SKILLS AND ENGLISH FOR ACADEMIC PURPOSES: A CASE STUDY OF A PROBLEM SHARED

SMILJKA GEE*, MICHAEL HUXLEY† and DUSKA JOHNSON*

*Lecturer, English Language Institute, University of Surrey
†Lecturer in Civil Engineering, University of Surrey

Introduction

In the 1981–82 session an unusually high proportion (about a quarter) of the students entering the Honours Degree course in Civil Engineering at the University of Surrey came from overseas. In fact, 17 students with average technical qualifications but with less than average ability in the English language were admitted. Section 1 of the paper gives some background information about the students and the demands of the first year course, which includes a course on Communication Skills. Section 2 gives details of an in-sessional language support programme and Section 3 describes the application of the language support to a report-writing exercise. Finally, some comments are made on the improvement in student performance over the year.

1. The Civil Engineering Course

1.1 The Students

The 17 students particularly referred to come from the Far East and the Middle East: 12 are from Hong Kong, Malaysia and China, and the remaining 5 from Iran, Jordan and Kuwait.

Prior to university entrance in October 1981, all but one of these students had studied A-levels at UK educational establishments. Apart from the extreme case of a student who had been a UK resident for more than ten years, the average length of pre-university residence was just over two years.

Selection for entry to the civil engineering course is based on A-level results in the mathematical and physical sciences. There was no statistically significant difference between the A-level qualifications of the overseas students and those of the remainder of the entrants to the course. In technical terms, therefore, they were amply qualified. In terms of their qualifications in the English language, however, they were undoubtedly deficient. Whereas the normal requirement for a home student is a pass in O-level English, none of the overseas students had reached a comparable standard. Their qualifications in English were all EFL qualifications (e.g. TOEFL, RSA, JMB) or qualifications given by their country of origin (e.g. Malaysian Certificate of Education, Abu Dhabi Local Examination), and their language difficulties were confirmed by the results of a diagnostic test.

1.2   Demands of the First-Year Civil Engineering Course

The first year of the undergraduate course in civil engineering is intensive. In an average week, students have about 25 timetabled contact hours, about half of which are accounted for by lecture periods. The remainder are made up of laboratory classes, tutorials and design work. In addition to the formal contact hours, students are expected to carry out a considerable amount of work in their own time.

The syllabus during the first session consists largely of subjects requiring skills of numeracy rather than of literacy. Despite this emphasis, proficiency in written English is important in a number of subjects: laboratory reports need to be written in a clearly-structured and concise fashion, and one subject (architectural forms) is examined solely by essay. Few of the native English-speaking students are particularly competent in essay and report-writing, and work in these areas presents problems for them, problems that are very much magnified for the overseas students. In an attempt to overcome or at least ease these difficulties, staff of the Civil Engineering Department run a course in Communication Skills during the first two terms of the first year. The course is attended by both home and overseas students.

1.3   The Communication Skills Course

Owing to the heavy academic load placed on first-year students, the length of the Communication Skills course is limited to 20 hours during the first two terms. Within this time it is not possible to cover the topic comprehensively, and the course concentrates on those three aspects which it is felt will be of most use to the students, viz. data presentation, report writing, and oral presentation. Other topics such as sketching and conduct of meetings are covered in less detail. Practical assignments occupy a large part of the course, and work submitted by the students is subjected to rigorous assessment. A high standard of attainment is expected, and frequently, written work is failed and returned for rewriting.

The first part of the course covers the selection of numerical and nonnumerical information for its relevance to the task in hand, its reduction to a readily-assimilated quantity, and its presentation via graphs, tables, and diagrams in a clear, legible and unambiguous fashion. Lessons learnt during this period are immediately applicable to the students' routine work, and form a necessary precursor to the later stages of the communication Skills course.

Technical report-writing is the second item on the course syllabus. Students are instructed on the functions of the various parts of a typical report (e.g. abstract, conclusions, appendix etc.) and are given advice on how to organize their approach to writing such a report. They are encouraged to learn by example, by reading engineering reports, and are recommended to buy and use one or more of the several instructional texts on report-writing that are currently available. No specific advice on writing correct English is given during this phase of the course although an appropriate bibliography is provided. Associated with this element of the course, during the latter half of the first university term, is a substantial assignment where the students are asked to produce a report on a realistic engineering problem. The assignment is deliberately designed to be a difficult exercise in communication. The particular exercise used during the 1981–82 session is described in some detail in 1.4 below.

The Communication Skills course ends with three sessions devoted to oral presentation. During the first session, before an audience comprising a member of staff and five fellow-students, each student gives a prepared talk lasting some five to seven minutes on a technical topic of his own choice. Various members of the audience are detailed to complete assessment forms on the speaker's performance or to make notes on the subject of the talk. The performance is recorded on video tape and the recording is played back immediately after the talk. After the playback the speaker has an opportunity for self-criticism, and the audience follow with their own reactions and suggestions for improvement. The second session is devoted to preparation for a further talk, with particular attention being paid to the preparation of visual aids and to correction of faults previously noted. In the last session the second performance is given to a larger audience, half of whom did not hear the first talk, and a further opportunity for feedback is given. This final part of the course is challenging and often frightening for the students, particularly for those from overseas. The results in terms of increased confidence and fluency of expression are, however, remarkable.

1.4 A Specific Communication Skills Assignment: 'The Skidding Problem'

Exercises during the Communication Skills course have been designed to be realistic, representing the sort of problem that might confront a civil engineer during his year of industrial training or shortly after graduation. In the 1981–82 session all of the students were required to complete a report-writing exercise entitled 'The Skidding Problem'.

For this exercise the student is asked to imagine that he is a new member of a County Highways Authority Accident Research Unit. A skidding accident has occurred at a local accident blackspot, and the authority may become involved in consequent litigation in which it is claimed that the road is unsafe. The Assistant County Surveyor has asked the student's boss (the head of the accident unit) for a report, and some preparatory work has been done. Unfortunately the head of the unit has fallen ill and will be out of action for two months, so the student has to write the report himself. He contacts the Assistant County Surveyor for clarification of his brief and is told that his report must cover three topics. He is asked to outline the important factors affecting skidding on roads, to give a brief interpretation of the data that the authority has on the accident site, and to give an opinion on whether accidents on the site follow a consistent pattern, i.e. whether the particular accident concerned was typical of those happening at the site and whether the authority may, therefore, lose the litigation.

Each student is given a set of materials containing:
  (i) a computer analysis of accidents at the site over a four-year period;
 (ii) a plan of the site showing locations of the accidents;
(iii) two research reports, and a portion of a third, dealing with the factors affecting skidding; and
(iv) a file, in date order, of memoranda and notes assembled by the head of the accident unit before his illness.

The reports serve a double purpose. Not only do they provide necessary information on the technical aspects of the problem, but they may also be used as models for structuring and presenting a report. Nearly all of the information given in the set of materials is genuine. The site referred to is an accident blackspot some 10 miles from the university, and the accident details are of real incidents on the site. Presentation of the accident data is in the same format as would be available to an employee of the responsible authority. To be consistent with the scenario presented to the students, however, some of the contents of the file of memoranda have been invented. The set of materials contains all the information necessary to enable the students to write the report, and much more besides. It is deliberately not neatly packaged, and the students need to spend some time on the assembly of pieces of information from various sources and on distinguishing relevant from irrelevant information.

The Skidding Problem exercise was developed bearing in mind that the engineering knowledge of students who are in their first term at university is slight. In fact, not much engineering background is required in order to complete the exercise successfully. There are, however, some technical terms involved that the students will not have met before, and these are thoroughly explained to them prior to their starting the exercise, to minimize hindrance caused by lack of technical understanding.

2. The Language Support Programme for Civil Engineering Students

2.1 Setting

Because of the significant number of overseas students whose language and study skills were inadequate for the course work they were required to do, it was clear that special measures would have to be taken. In the assessment of the exercises in Communication Skills (which are difficult even for home students) and of essay-type examinations such as architectural forms, no special concessions are made for those whose English is poor. There was a danger that some of the overseas students would fail to survive academically, not because of lack of potential in their specialist subject, but simply as a result of language difficulties.

There was therefore a need for a language support programme in addition to the Communication Skills course. It was run by English specialist staff in liaison with staff of the Civil Engineering Department. The programme was in-sessional, designed to provide tuition and practice in planning and structuring discourse, organizing information obtained from a variety of sources, expressing and presenting knowledge of the subject matter clearly and correctly in speech or in writing — in short, the language and study skills which were essential for carrying out the study tasks required by the Civil Engineering Department.

Although the in-sessional nature of the language support programme made it possible for English tutors to relate the students' language needs directly to their academic needs, it also imposed some constraints on the structure and organization of language teaching. The time available for language work was restricted, since the students were studying full-time on their degree course. The coursework required by the Civil Engineering Department had to be completed within specified time limits, which could not be extended to allow for the intensive language support the students needed in order to reach adequate standards. It was therefore necessary to design a language support programme which provided tuition and practice in relevant language and study skills, using as little student time as possible. In these circumstances, the primary objective of the programme had to be to help the students cope with their subject workload, while keeping to a minimum the requirements of the language course itself.

With this in mind, the language support programme was based on an analysis of both language and academic needs. Cooperation with subject-specialist staff was required in order to determine the areas of the degree course where language problems were most likely to affect academic performance, to specify language and study skills most relevant to the academic requirements of the degree course, and to define the target level of competence necessary for achieving the standard of academic performance expected by the subject-specialist staff.

2.2 Course Structure

The language support course involved analysis of three main types of written assignment: technical report, essay, and essay-type exam answers, selected in consultation with subject-specialist staff. (In addition, language support was also given with organization and presentation of talks and writing of laboratory reports, which the students requested.)

Analysis of Assignments

Each assignment was broken down into ordered tasks, used by students as guidelines for both the global structure of the assignment and the procedure to follow in the course of their work. For example, the assignment 'outline the important factors affecting skidding' (Part 1 of the technical report: 'The Skidding Problem')* consists of the following tasks.

1. Writing a brief outline of what the students already know about skidding. For example: 'Skidding occurs when a vehicle slips on the road, out of control because of slippery road or faulty tyres'.

2. Selecting reference texts (from the set of materials given by the Civil Engineering Department), and dividing this material into three main sections to provide an outline of the global structure of the report. For example: (a) slipperiness of a road
    (b) tyre properties
    (c) interaction of tyre and road

3. Reading and note-taking: selecting only the information relevant to the topic of the assignment (important factors affecting skidding).

4. Organizing information in terms of report structure, using a reference text as a model. For example:
   Factors affecting skidding
   1.   Factors affecting the slipperiness of a road surface
   1.1 Wet and dry conditions
   1.2 Road surface
   1.3 Contamination of the road surface

5. Describing briefly each numbered section: writing up notes, summarizing reference texts, incorporating diagrams, tables, etc.

6. Checking that the descriptions are coherent, and correcting language errors.

Specification of Linguistic Requirements

The language content was specified in terms of:

(i) language and study skills necessary for carrying out the tasks, such as:
   ● understanding basic discourse structure (topic, development,

---

*Details of the language support programme for the major written assignment — 'The Skidding Problem' — are given in Section 3.

transition, conclusion) and its use for skimming to obtain the gist of the text
- searching for specific information in a text
- structuring discourse (introducing discourse topic, giving examples/reasons/details, concluding the topic)
- developing basic reference skills, such as use of headings, numbering, indentation
- relating information presented in diagrams or tables to written discourse

(ii) language functions and structures such as:
- expressing referential relationships using articles and pronouns
- expressing comments and opinions using modal verbs
- adding information using elements of sentence structure (subordination, embedding)
- punctuation

2.3 Selection of Teaching Materials

Bibliographies and other relevant materials were provided by the subject-specialist staff, and were used by students as main reference texts, supplementary materials and models for the organization and presentation of their own work.

Some grading of the materials in terms of linguistic complexity was necessary, to ensure that all relevant materials, however difficult, could be understood and used by the students. Specially designed worksheets were prepared by language teaching staff for dealing with comprehension problems.

2.4 Organization of Teaching

The teaching was carried out in the form of:
(i) group discussions, especially in the initial stages of the work when the assignments were analysed and tasks explained;
(ii) workshops, where the students worked on their own reports, with language tutors monitoring their progress, helping with individual difficulties, explaining the use of specific language items, etc.; and
(iii) tutorials, which were arranged as necessary
  (a) with subject-specialist staff to deal with problems related to understanding of the subject-matter; and
  (b) with language tutors to deal with problems of presentation, organization and with language problems in general.

2.5 Discussion of the programme

A similar course structure to that outlined in 2.2 was used in the work on all three assignments selected by the teaching staff. Since the programme thus covered a range of assignments, using the same basic structure with the same set of tasks, the students received sufficient practice in relevant language and study skills without having to do language work for its own sake.

Student motivation was therefore high, both with respect to the subject-matter (which they found 'interesting, useful and understandable') and the language work (because they understood 'why it was necessary to know the English language well'). Another factor that contributed to student motivation was the flexibility in the organization of teaching, which allowed them to work at their own pace. As the students came from a variety of educational backgrounds and their levels of proficiency in English varied, the flexibility of the course also allowed each student to concentrate on the tasks that he found the most difficult, while skipping some less difficult ones.

3. Language Support for 'The Skidding Problem'

Since in the Communication Skills course the students were instructed on how to structure and organize reports in general rather than being taught the specific skills of report-writing, the primary aim of the language programme was to enable them to carry out the coursework. The programme was designed to teach the necessary back-up language and study skills, and therefore its nature was that of support.

In planning the support programme for 'The Skidding Problem' assignment, special attention was given to establishing a step-by-step working procedure, so that the reports satisfied the criteria used by the Civil Engineering staff.

3.1   Criteria for Assessment

In the assessment of the students' attempts at the assignment, the following aspects were considered.

  (i) Scope and layout:
     Did the report fulfil the requirements of the brief without including irrelevant or unimportant detail? Did it have a clear and logical structure, following a conventional order, and was it complete with title page, abstract, table of contents, references etc?

  (ii) Style:
     Was the report written in a clear, fluent and appropriate style of English? Was it brief, as required, and did the essential facts and arguments stand out?

  (iii) Presentation:
     Was the report clearly and attractively presented?
     Did it make the reader want to read it?

  (iv) Use of English:
     Was the English grammatically correct? Were there spelling mistakes?

(v) Technical Content:
   Was the technical content of the report accurate, and was the opinion given consistent with the facts?

Of these points, the first four were considered to be of prime importance. Minor technical errors were corrected and forgiven because of the students' unfamiliarity with the subject.

3.2   Course Description: 'The Skidding Problem'

The course was divided into stages dealing with the planning, organization and structuring of the report, gathering of information, and writing-up.

The starting point of each stage involved analysis and interpretation of the tasks, and these were accompanied by setting out the procedures for the students to follow in order to complete the tasks.

Stage 1

The aim was to work out the structure of the report within the very strict conventions of technical report-writing. In working out the outline of the report, the students made constant reference to the model of a technical report provided by the Department of Civil Engineering, and translated the requirements and specifications of the report into the conventional report structure.

The students were involved in the following tasks:
   (i) analysis and interpretation of the assignment as a whole; and
   (ii) working out the global outline of the report.

The skills needed for these tasks were: reading skills (for example scanning and skimming); reference skills (for example understanding and use of graphic presentation, table of contents, index); study skills (for example note-taking, outlining); and writing skills (for example rephrasing, summarizing).

Stage 2

The aim of this stage was to collect the information to be included in the report, and to organize it into the structure of the report as outlined in Stage 1. The tasks were:
   (i) outlining each part of the report;
   (ii) locating and selecting information; and
   (iii) planning and organizing information.

The tasks required the same set of skills as in Stage 1, and some additional ones in order to locate and select specific information. These included: discriminating relevant from irrelevant information; distinguishing main ideas from supporting details; transcoding information in diagrams, tables etc.

Stage 3

The aim was to put together the selected information and write up the report. The tasks carried out were to:

(i) organize the information into expository language;

(ii) formulate the engineer's point of view in the conclusion of the report; and

(iii) write an abstract, include references.

This stage required a number of writing skills such as summarizing, rephrasing, expressing own ideas, making references etc. Furthermore, it required organization of information into paragraph structure. Basic paragraph structure (topic, development, transition, conclusion) was taught and practised in the writing of the entire report. Some errors in sentence structure (especially with coordination and subordination) had to be corrected, as well as frequent grammatical and spelling mistakes. A major problem at this point was the impending deadline for submission, and as a result some students did not complete the necessary language work in time.

3.3   Teaching

An important aspect of the work was discussion. It was most prominent in the preliminary stages, especially when discussing the litigation, and the consequences the report was likely to have on its outcome.

The students were encouraged to discuss and exchange ideas and to put forward their own views. They were actively involved in all stages of the work. They were involved in problem-solving exercises with the aim of establishing why they were doing a particular task and what it involved. The role of the teacher was to offer guidance and help when necessary, and to teach those skills which were needed for successful completion of the work. In addition, the students' progress was monitored and checked at all times, and any obstacles and difficulties were immediately removed.

While the preliminary stages of the work were done in the class, most of the writing-up was done in tutorials. The reason for this was that it was felt that individual errors were best discussed and corrected in a tutorial situation. Furthermore, additional remedial work on specific areas of difficulty was also done in these sessions.

The students' motivation was high, partly because their progress was closely monitored and as a result they were able to move smoothly from one stage to the next, and partly because the report was part of the degree-course work and therefore more meaningful.

4. Results and Discussion

It is not possible to compare the performance of the overseas students who received language support with results obtained by a set of overseas students who did not, since no such set exists. Their performance can, however, be compared with that of the home students following the same course.

4.1 Performance on 'The Skidding Problem' (technical report-writing)

This assignment was assessed at the end of the first term, and the results obtained by the overseas students were considerably lower than those of home students. Five overseas students (but only two home students) failed, and were asked to re-write sections of the report.

Subsequent review of the programme indicated that failure was in part attributable to the very strict deadline. The major factor contributing to lack of time, however, was the students' lack of experience in organizing and structuring their work, so much so that many students needed six or seven weeks to structure their reports, leaving only one week for writing and for correcting language errors.

4.2 Performance on Architectural Forms (essay writing)

The problems with organization and structure, which were so important in the first term, were by this time largely overcome, and so much more time was available for language work and correction.

Results achieved in this subject, examined at the end of the second term, were very encouraging. The highest mark was awarded jointly to four candidates, of whom three were overseas students participating in the language programme. As a group, the overseas students obtained average marks almost 5% higher than those of the remainder of the class. A test indicates this difference to be significant at the 5% level (i.e. there was less than a 1 in 20 chance of the observed difference occurring in random sampling).

4.3 End-of-session Examination Performance

The results of the overseas students in the end-of-session examinations were distinguishable from those of the home students in only one respect: none of them failed the year's examinations completely, whereas five of the home students did. The average marks awarded to home and overseas students in

CG–E*

the year's examinations were virtually identical, as consideration of their pre-entry technical qualifications alone might have suggested.

Acknowledgements

The authors are indebted to:

- Peter Gardiner, Senior Lecturer in Highway Engineering, for devising 'The Skidding Problem', for giving generously of his time in assessing it, and for his continuing enthusiasm and support for the Communication Skills course.

- Henry Rosenberg, Lecturer-in-Charge of the English Language Programme, for his support and encouragement.

- Pauline Wadsworth for typing the paper.

Editor's Comment

This paper describes an excellent example of close collaboration between two specialist fields: EFL and Civil Engineering. The procedure described incorporates the essential elements of such teaching, viz.

- willingness to collaborate on the part of both sets of staff
- clear demarcation as to where their respective responsibilities lie
- awareness of each other's conceptual apparatus and teaching approach
- the joint effort being viewed by the student as a complementary teaching situation

Readers who wish to explore further case-studies in collaborative teaching should consult *ELT Documents 106 — Team Teaching in ESP*, London: The British Council. A case-study of collaborative teaching in L1 is to be found in Jackson M. and Price J. (1981) 'A way forward: a fusion of two cultures', in *ELT Documents 112 — The ESP Teacher: Role, Development and Prospects*, London: The British Council.

RCW

THE TEAM TEACHING OF WRITING SKILLS

TONY DUDLEY-EVANS

University of Birmingham

Introduction

An important feature of the work of the English for Overseas Students Unit at the University of Birmingham is team-teaching of overseas postgraduate students in various departments with large numbers of such students. This approach has involved the working together in the same classroom of a language teacher and a subject teacher to meet students' needs in the following areas:

a) lecture comprehension
b) writing examination answers

The work on lecture comprehension has involved the language teacher recording subject lectures and then preparing a handout which checks both understanding of the main and subsidiary points presented in the lecture, and of the technical, semi-technical and colloquial vocabulary used by the lecturer. The handout then forms the basis for the team-taught session, in which the language teacher and the subject teacher work together to help students with specific problems arising from the lecture.

The work on writing examination answers follows a similar pattern. The subject teacher chooses a typical examination question from his own field. The meaning of the question, and the expectations of the examiner who set the question are then discussed by the students, which in turn leads into a discussion of a possible plan for the answer. This discussion is guided by the language teacher, and commented upon by the subject teacher. (For a full description of this work see Johns and Dudley-Evans, 1980, and Dudley-Evans and Johns, 1981.)

Similar work involving lecture comprehension and essay writing was initiated at Ngee Ann Polytechnic, an English medium institute in Singapore (Dudley-Evans, 1981). However, it became apparent that such work aimed at meeting students' academic needs in following their college courses needed to be complemented by materials designed to develop the students' writing skills when they entered employment. In Singapore, where English is used extensively in government and business, the ability to communicate effectively both orally and in writing is essential. Thus the Building

Department, whose graduates have a particularly strong need for writing skills, in particular report-writing skills, requested the English Language Unit to run a course in report writing in the final year of their three-year course. The English Language Unit suggested that the course be team-taught by members of the Building Department and the English Language Unit, and this was accepted by the Department. It is the purpose of this paper to describe the course, in the hope that it will be of interest and relevance to those concerned with overseas students and with 'communication' courses for native speakers in polytechnics and technical colleges.

1. Background

Ngee Ann Polytechnic provides three-year diploma courses in mechanical engineering, electrical and electronic engineering, shipbuilding repair technology, building maintenance and management, and business studies. Students normally enter the college after O-level, but A-level students are now accepted for a two-year course leading to the same diploma. This diploma is largely equivalent to the Higher National Diploma (HND) taken in British technical colleges and polytechnics, and diploma holders are normally exempted from the first year of a BSc course.

The Building Maintenance and Management course is designed to prepare students for work in the areas of maintenance of services in housing estates, or in estate management. In the first two years of the three-year course, students are given a background in basic areas such as construction of buildings, mechanical and electrical services, property management and law. In the final year, students are divided into two groups: one concerned with estate management and the other with maintenance of services. The management programme includes courses in property law, property valuation and economics, while the maintenance programme concentrates on air-conditioning, building automation and the maintenance of mechanical and electrical services.

This, then, is the background to the final-year English course, referred to in the Introduction, which was designed to prepare students for as many as possible of the writing tasks that students may have to carry out in their future jobs.

2. Syllabus for the Course

The list of writing-tasks to be covered in the course was drawn up by the subject teachers involved, in consultation with the language teachers. These tasks are:

(i) *Specification Writing*
This involves the management students in writing full specifications for a cleaning contract for a private estate, and the maintenance students in writing specifications for the installation of a new air-conditioning unit.

(ii) *Memo-writing*
This involves the writing of memos giving instructions for the repair of building faults. An important part of this section of the course gives suggestions on how to vary language according to whom the memo is being sent. It aims at making students aware of the differences in style required when writing to a superior, a peer, or a subordinate. It also aims at making students aware of the dangers of using very formal and rather abrupt language when writing to the general public.

(iii) *Case-Study and Recommendations on Action to be taken*
Students are given a case-study based on likely situations arising in property management. They have to decide on action to be taken, and write a full report recommending this action.

(iv) *Accident Reports*
Students write a report describing the events of an accident (shown on video) and make recommendations about the prevention of similar accidents.

(v) *Progress Reports*
Students write reports on an imaginary project. In particular, they report to senior management on 'work-in-hand'.

(vi) *Interpretation of Replies to a Questionnaire*
Students make inferences from a set of data, and write a full report on the data.

(vii) *Purchase Order*
Students are given an imaginary situation, for which they have to order equipment from relevant catalogues.

(viii) *Reports on Meetings*
Students listen to a simulated site meeting and write the minutes of the meeting. They are then written up as if to be sent to their senior management.

(ix) *A Full Report*
As part of the course, students have to write a full report: a valuation report in the case of management students, a technical report on lifts in the case of maintenance students.

3. Methodology

In the writing of materials and in the planning of the teaching, our procedure has been as follows. The subject teacher has normally found an authentic situation for exploitation, or has devised a situation that could well occur in reality (what we might call a semi-authentic situation), and produced a model report on that situation. Before the class, the language teacher has usually discussed the model report with the subject teacher, and decided on the language points to be highlighted.

In the teaching of the material the language teacher has usually played the dominant role, leading the discussion about the writing of the report, the points to be included, and ways of expressing these points. The subject teacher acts as a consultant on matters of content, and comments on the appropriacy of students' answers. There are times, however, when the subject teacher will take over the dominant role, especially where aspects of the situation need to be explained in some detail. Most pieces of writing are marked by both, and content and language are given equal weighting.

The actual teaching strategies have varied according to the nature of the task. Where possible, the strategy has been to:

a) Present the situation and ask students to work out a plan for reporting on it. This is often done in pairs or groups.

b) Discuss as a class the various plans worked out by groups.

c) Write up the report.

d) Receive feedback from subject and language teachers on these reports.

e) Present a model, which is either written by the subject teacher or based on the best of the work produced by the class.

f) Give other students other related situations, and ask them to adapt the model presented for these new situations.

This approach is clearly different from the Presentation, Practice and Production methodology common in language teaching. It is, however, quite similar to various suggestions for appropriate methodology for communicative language teaching, especially Brumfit (1980) (Figure 1):

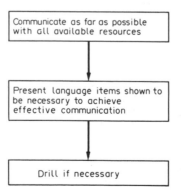

For a number of tasks, however, it would be very difficult for students to work out a plan without some pre-guidance from the teachers, because of lack of experience of either the content, or of the language to be used. For example, in the case of writing specifications (item (i) in the above list of tasks) it was clear that students had had no experience of writing specifications and probably very little experience of even reading them. Therefore, before they could practice writing, they had to:

a) understand the purpose of specifications

b) recognize the various types of specifications

c) be given guidance about appropriate style for specifications, such as whether to use the shall + passive form (e.g. The floor shall be finished with . . .) or the imperative form (e.g. Finish the floor with . . .).

After the students had been taken through these steps, they were given an example of a specification document, which they analysed in some detail before adapting it for use in a related situation. Thus the teaching unit began with a description of the purpose of a type of writing, followed by analysis of an example of that writing, leading to the adaptation of that example for a new situation.

This same procedure was used in preparing students to write valuation reports. Such a procedure is, we believe, reasonably realistic in that a manager would be unlikely to undertake a major task like the writing of specifications or a valuation report without consulting previous examples. The vital skill is to be able to select those parts relevant to the task in hand and to omit other parts.

As mentioned in the syllabus outline, students are required to write a large-scale report as part of the course, and for a certain period classes are cancelled to enable students to carry out the necessary research and investigation. By undertaking and writing up a project of this type with the help of both subject and language teachers (usually in a tutorial where individual problems can best be handled) students gain valuable experience of how to set about a full-scale project report. To put it very simply, students at this level (intermediate to advanced) best learn to write by writing and then receiving feedback on what they have done, and rewriting as appropriate.

4. General Considerations

Two main issues emerge from the above description of the syllabus and the methodology. One concerns the validity of the amount of prescription about the language to be used, and the other the value of team-teaching in English for Occupational Purposes.

5. Prescription

The course is at times quite prescriptive about both the organization of reports and the language to be used, and the question arises as to whether the amount of prescription can be justified. We would argue that it *is* justified, for two reasons:

a) The suggestions about organization and language are based on the experience of the subject lecturer, and, wherever possible, on the analysis of the kind of writing expected of managers in the building and property industry.

b) It is never suggested that the guidance about organisation and language represents the only way of approaching the given writing task. Indeed, it is made clear that there are other ways of approaching the task.

We would propose that for any writing course of this type and at the level described, it is necessary both to give models that may be adapted for use in different situations, and to expose students to a repertoire of relevant language forms that can be used as required.

6. Value of Team-Teaching in English for Occupational Purposes

In the description of team-teaching at the University of Birmingham referred to at the beginning of this paper (Johns and Dudley-Evans, 1980), we suggested that an overseas student's inability to cope with his subject course is rarely the result of his lack of 'knowledge of subject' or his lack of 'knowledge of language' by themselves; it is more often the result of the intertwining of these two factors. Thus, if language and subject work are totally separate it is very difficult to tackle the problem effectively and to take account of this intertwining. We also suggested that in the triangle of which the three angles are the students, the subject teacher and the language teacher, each needs assistance and feedback from the other two. The subject teacher needs feedback on how effectively he is communicating with his students, and on whether his assumptions about the level at which to present a particular topic are justified or not. The language teacher needs to understand something of the conceptual framework of the subjects his students are studying, and to observe at first hand where students encounter difficulties with their subject course. The student needs feedback on how well he is meeting the expectations of the course, and needs assistance with difficulties as they arise.

When, however, we are dealing with English for Occupational Purposes, one needs to make a distinction between pre-experience and post-experience. The student already engaged in his profession should be able to assess fairly clearly his needs in English and his weaknesses in communication. He is likely to have had experience of the communicative tasks taught in the course, and to be aware of his problems in performing that task. In such cases the need for a course team-taught with a subject teacher may be less strong. Where, however, the course is *pre*-experience, students are unlikely to have had experience of the communicative tasks to be taught, and one will not have the opportunity to draw on students' knowledge and experience. Thus the need for a team-taught course is very strong, and the role of the subject teacher is crucial.

The pre-experience team-taught EOP course therefore needs close co-operation between the subject teacher and the language teacher. It needs joint planning of the aims of the course, the syllabus, the relationship between the subject content and the language input, the preparation of models for different types of writing, and the methods of assessment. It also needs careful co-ordination of lesson preparation and marking of written work. All of this takes place outside the classroom. Inside the classroom it is necessary to ensure that both the teachers themselves and the students understand the different roles of the teachers, and whether the focus of a given part of the lesson is on subject or on language.

7. Conclusions

It is a little early to evaluate the course described in this paper; this will only be possible once the students have entered employment and are able to give feedback to the college of the effectiveness of the writing course. In the meantime, it is possible to report that the co-operation between the language teacher and the subject teacher has worked and that their different contributions have dovetailed well. Particularly important is the fact that both have worked together as equals, each aware of and respecting the contribution of the other. We would hope that our experience is of relevance to any teaching programme from which students will enter jobs in which communication in English is vital.

Notes

1. I should like to express my gratitude to Don Hampton, Mrs Grace Quah, Lesley Goh and Toh Eng Kheem of the Building Department, and Ms Heather Lotherington of the English Language Unit, who taught on the first year of the course described in this paper.
2. This paper is an adapted version of Paper 9 in a collection of papers presented as part of a submission by the author for an Official Degree of the University of Birmingham, in May 1982.

References

BRUMFIT, C. J. *Problems and Principles in English Teaching*, Oxford: Pergamon, 1980.
DUDLEY-EVANS, A. 'Towards Team Teaching', *English Language Research Journal* No 2, University of Birmingham, 1981.
DUDLEY-EVANS, A. and JOHNS, T. F. 'A Team Teaching Approach to Lecture Comprehension for Overseas Students', in *The Teaching of Listening Comprehension*, ELT Documents Special. London: The British Council, 1981.
JOHNS, T. F. and DUDLEY-EVANS, A. 'An Experiment in Team Teaching of Overseas Postgraduate Students of Transportation and Plant Biology', in *ELT Documents 106: Team Teaching in ESP*, London: The British Council, 1980.

Editor's Comment

Although this paper is written by one of the best-known ESP textbook writers, the situation it describes is more typical of that found in Communication Skills courses, given that many students at Ngee Ann Polytechnic in Singapore may often have a written competence in English similar to their equivalents in British Technical Institutions. All the same, a regularized team-teaching approach to assisting the students develop their linguistic and communicative skills is one that is particularly associated with ESP (de Escorcia and Gee, Huxley and Johnson in this volume; and the references cited in this paper). But because the courses described by Dudley-Evans are *occupational* and because the students are speakers of English as a second rather than a foreign language, this paper should be of considerable interest to those concerned with developing first-language Communication Skills courses.

JMS

TEAM-TEACHING FOR STUDENTS OF ECONOMICS: A COLOMBIAN EXPERIENCE

BLANCA A. DE ESCORCIA

Universidad del Valle, Cali, Colombia

Introduction

One of the main activities of the Languages Department at the Universidad del Valle is to design and teach ESP courses to support the multiplicity of degree courses that contain an English-language requirement. Thus, the Department has produced over the last few years materials for different programmes in the natural sciences, including several branches of engineering, the health sciences, the basic sciences and education. Programmes in the social sciences have not received so much attention from the Department due mainly to the fact that they are a relatively small part of the over-all University programme, and also because of the general belief that English does not play such a central role as an instrument of access to specialized bibliography in this area.

The Economics Programme makes provision for two courses of English (of 80 hours each), offered in the first two semesters of an eight-semester degree. For reasons that will not be discussed here, the entering students must be considered as false beginners, as reflected in their poor performance in the English placement examination administered in their first week of class.

Until recently, there were no set criteria or specific teaching materials for the English for Economics courses. It was up to the teacher to adopt whatever approach he thought adequate, and to use readily-available textbooks or make his own selection of readings as he went along. There was only one requirement: reading comprehension was to be the aim of the courses, since it has been widely shown by several surveys (e.g. Lopez and Conover, 1980) that reading is considered the most useful and necessary skill in all academic subjects at the University.

In 1980 a decision was made to introduce experimentally the series *Reading and Thinking in English* (1979) in different programmes at the University where specific materials had not yet been produced. It was thought that the series would be a good introduction to the reading skills necessary for academic purposes. The initial reaction of the students was favourable. They felt they had something to learn from the methodology used in the series, and their reading strategies improved. In economics, however, *Reading and*

Thinking in English proved to be less acceptable to the students and was seriously objected to in the second semester of its use. It should be said at this point that English in Economics has generally been considered simply as an academic requirement; if it had any instrumental value, this was potential rather than actual, i.e. a possibly useful tool at the post-graduate level. The attitude of the staff tends to reinforce this feeling of postponement, since most teachers do not read English fluently and tend to favour academic reading in Spanish for themselves and for their students. In other words, although everybody feels that it is 'good for you' to know English, the immediate relevance of its use is not manifested, and strong demands to read references in English are seldom made. It is therefore interesting to note that it was the *students* who started a move for more relevance in the English courses. The series being used was felt to be useful, but its content irrelevant for economists; and, as a result of long and fruitful discussions with the students, the idea of a team-teaching approach was proposed by the teacher (myself) to remedy the difficult situation that had emerged.

1.   Planning Considerations

In February 1982 I made a proposal to the Head of the Languages Department to initiate a team-teaching project for economics freshmen starting their first semester in March 1982. Decisions are often made on the spot in our Department, and the lack of a reasonable period of time to organize the project did not seem to matter. This hasty decision, however, forced me to accept conditions which were quite unfavourable in terms of the project, leading to crucial changes in my original plans.

In the first semester, students take four main subjects, besides English: Principles of Economics I, Introduction to Social Doctrines I, Introduction to the Colombian Economy, and Mathematics. Of these, Principles of Economics seemed to be the most obvious candidate for subject-specialist collaboration. It is considered to be the main subject of the first-semester courses, and is followed up by a sequence of related courses in the following semesters. The teacher (henceforth BS) was contacted and he expressed his willingness to co-operate, although he showed surprise at the fact that a subject such as English should be given such a considerable amount of attention. In fact, he himself has a working knowledge of the language, but the Economics Literature he uses and recommends is in Spanish, mostly translations of the original English-language sources which are reproduced as mimeographed handouts.

After this initial contact with the subject teacher, an outline of the project was drawn up, setting out the conditions for teamwork. Unfortunately, for administrative reasons, timetables could not be arranged to make it possible for us to attend each other's classes. This condition, which I had considered essential for the development of the project, had to be discarded from the beginning, causing radical changes to be introduced as far as the content matter of the materials was concerned. The fact that a strictly parallel course could not be developed also altered some methodological assumptions previously accepted for team-teaching projects (Skehan, 1980). However, some of these constraints turned out to be 'blessings in disguise'.

2. Stages of the Project

2.1 Studying the Programme of the Parallel Course

After having established that the collaboration between the team members would be rather loose, due originally to external administrative reasons, several meetings were held with BS to discuss the general outline of the course. The link would be established through the content matter of the Principles of Economics course, which defined its objectives as

". . . to introduce the student to the fundamental aspects of economic thought. The objective is not to present the history of economic doctrines, but to study the central issues of certain schools. Value and distribution will be the points of departure for the discussion, and an attempt will be made to show how these problems originated and how they were interpreted and redefined by each economic school or author".

A careful study of the programme was carried out jointly to determine the topics to be included in the English course. The main topics isolated for consideration were: the Mercantilist and Physiocratic Schools; the origins of classical economics; and the concepts of value, price and distribution as developed by Smith and Ricardo.

I would like, at this point, to make it clear that an important theoretical decision was made. Since one of the main characteristics of the Social Sciences is to deal with ideas and the expression of values rather than with facts (especially in the type of course we are discussing here), it seems that a strictly parallel course in English is impossible and probably undesirable. It is impossible for two main reasons.

1) The exposition of ideas will depend on the characteristics of the teacher himself, his own beliefs, and his own position and attitude towards the particular issues discussed.

2) Participation in the economics class will involve extensive reading (in Spanish) leading to class discussion and exchange of ideas, whereas the English class (at level I) can only hope to handle short texts as intensive reading. Thus, the amount of material discussed in the 'Principles of Economics' class could never be matched in the English class.

Further, strict parallelism is probably undesirable in this type of course because of the very nature of the discussion itself. The social sciences involve a great deal of personal interpretation. A parallel course will best serve its purpose by presenting the sources which originate discussion, and thus allow the students to arrive at their own interpretations as an alternative source of ideas to those expounded in the specialized class. The principle adopted here is to recreate in the English class the types of problems and discussions that the student will encounter in the specialist class situation, and to try and find solutions to the problems through the English texts.

2.2 Drawing a General Outline of the English Programme

Due to the pressure of time, decisions had to be made very quickly as to the way in which the economics discourse would be handled for pedagogic presentation. No systematic study of this type of discourse was on hand, so any approach adopted would be quite arbitrary. At a macro-level of organization, however, I decided to break away radically from some of the traditions attached to most of our ESP courses:

● The emphasis would be exclusively on the development of reading skills, and no formal grammatical component would be handled as such, unless the students specifically asked for this kind of support in particularly difficult passages. Some of the main sources of difficulty in the interpretation of scientific texts (nominal constructions, passive forms, for example) do not seem to be as widely used in the social sciences, which handle a more explicit straightforward type of argumentation, very similar in linguistic structure, as it turned out, to the corresponding discourse in Spanish. (This point will be taken up again later.)

● Before getting into the study of the specialized texts as such, I felt there was a need for an introductory unit on those very basic reading strategies which are usually taken for granted in other courses. This unit turned out to be a most successful way to introduce the students to English 'without fear'.

● The content and organization of the rest of the course would be decided as work progressed in the parallel course, and as a more detailed examination of the types of discourse involved could be undertaken.

3. Methodology

It seems to me that the aim of any foreign-language course should be to help the learners develop a capacity to handle normal language situations in a manner similar to what they would do in their native language. A possible way of doing this is to provide them with an adequate number of models of the language representing authentic situations in which they will find themselves in real life. However, in order to overcome the problems of linguistic complexity typical of authentic texts, a methodology needs to be developed taking into account familiarity with the subject-matter and the manner of presentation of the topics to be discussed. The methodology for this course was developed taking the following parameters into consideration:

1) *Content*   This should follow as closely as possible the topics discussed in the parallel course. The selection of reading passages should be made preferably from the bibliography recommended by the subject-specialist teacher. BS only recommended Spanish translations for his course, but he provided me with additional reading lists in English. Among the books

recommended were, on the one hand, primary sources (works by classical economists) and, on the other hand, commentaries, historical accounts and critical essays related to the original sources.

2) *Presentation*   Some criterion for the organization of the units had to be found. Systematization is the most crucial element in any methodological attempt at organizing teaching materials. Exposure to any kind of problem, whether linguistic, conceptual, functional or otherwise must be multiple before learning can be fruitfully achieved. In the time available, a detailed discourse analysis of economics texts was impossible, but a quick survey of a large number of the recommended references yielded the following preliminary results:

● A good deal of the work of the social scientist is based on the discussion and critical evaluation of somebody else's ideas. This type of work generates a large number of texts where authors or schools of thought or concepts are compared and evaluated. Comparison and contrast is therefore one of the main discoursal activities in economics.

● In the texts describing historical events or characterizing particular historical periods, generalizations are made about social structure and organization.

● As in other types of texts, prediction plays a fundamental role in the structure of economics discourse (Tadros, 1980). However, one particular form of prediction (reporting) plays a particularly crucial role in commentaries and critical appraisals.

4. Course Content

As a result of these observations, teaching units were organized as follows:

Unit I: General reading strategies
Unit II: Basic functions (comparison and contrast, prediction, generalization)
Unit III: Expressing opinions and reporting an author's ideas.

This division into units simply constitutes a useful schema for distributing the students' work throughout the semester. Although the basic functions as expressed by the title serve as a basis for text selection, many other issues (linguistic and non-linguistic) emerge in class presentation and discussion. Each of these Units is now briefly described.

Unit I

The purpose of this unit is to introduce the students to a different outlook on what a foreign language is and how it can be handled. Some of the misconceptions that the student develops throughout secondary school have to be counteracted. The usual attitude towards English texts is one of fear and mistrust. Although over 67% of the University library books are in English (54% in the case of economics), very few students consult them with any regularity, especially in the first semesters of their careers. Only some of the members of staff and final semester students use English-medium texts on a regular basis. If I want students to become readers of English, they have to familiarize themselves with English books and periodicals. Skills on how to use the library, making a survey of English books, checking out and exploring the different parts of a book, guessing the contents from the title and other markers, looking at the index and making sense of it, etc. were some of the activities that broke the ice from the beginning, and made my freshmen students the most regular customers at the library counter. Another tradition was broken: the students actually asked the other teachers (including BS) to provide them with additional references in English for their courses. Thus, throughout the semester, the students were the main link between the parallel course and the English class, showing in this way that the interest towards the foreign language came also from them and was not an imposition by the English teacher. Another important development of this introduction to the handling of reading material was the fact that they were able later on to work on individual reading projects—including the selection of a text of their choice, the interpretation of a fragment of the text, and the writing of a summary in Spanish—achievements which are not usually expected from first-semester students in the English class.

A further outcome of Unit I was the realization that understanding the words as isolated units and being able to make adequate word-by-word translations into Spanish does not guarantee a correct interpretation of the text. Vocabulary is usually thought to be the problem in technical discourse, but even in those cases where most words have corresponding Spanish cognates and where the structure of the text is quite straightforward, it is not immediately obvious what the conceptual meaning of the passage may be. This is specially true in the social sciences, where everyday words and expressions take on specialized meanings. (Compare, for example, the common and specialized meanings of terms such as *value, price, utility* and *distribution.*) Guessing meaning from the context, using the dictionary adequately, and providing their own background knowledge were strategies that the students learned to handle efficiently in their interpretation of the English texts.

Unit II

Two principles of organization were considered in the order of presentation: content and rhetorical function. No chronological order is respected in the sequencing of the topics, since in the discussion of concepts in the social sciences, incursions are made back and forth in time, introducing bits of information from other periods and other related schools of thought. Adam Smith is thus the centre of attention, but texts on the Mercantilist and the Physiocratic schools are included at different points in the unit as part of the general historical, social and economic background of the period. These topics reflect quite closely the organization of the parallel course. Linguistic and rhetorical criteria, on the other hand, were selected as principles for systematization in the handling of the language. *Comparison and contrast* was found to be one of the main discoursal activities in texts relating to this area. Thus, we find texts comparing the social organization of two different countries or the main ideas of two schools of thought; authors are compared as to their postulates and their styles of writing; forms of trade, types of economic policies, and concepts such as *value* are also compared. Of course, a wide range of linguistic devices is used to express comparison and contrast: syntactic, lexical, textual. No attempt was made to give priority to one type of structure over another, and the students were encouraged to recognize any elements, grammatical or otherwise, that might be fulfilling a comparative purpose.

Ways in which economics authors announce to their readers what is to come was a second functional area given detailed attention in this Unit. Three of Tadros' (1981) categories seemed particularly important: *enumeration, advance labelling* and *reporting*. However, I found that *reporting* played such an important role in texts dealing with the development of ideas that I decided to make *reporting* the main theme of the third Unit.

Unit III

In the organization of this unit, content and linguistic organization were again taken into account. The parallel Principles of Economics course was beginning work on Ricardo and his theory of value and distribution, so I chose this topic as central to the content of the Unit. From the discoursal point of view, *reporting*, both direct and indirect, was the main criterion in the selection. Part of the unit deals with the expression of opinion and evaluation by the author, a most productive theme that I intend to explore further.

This Unit turned out to have significant pedagogical implications for the team-teaching project, since the topics discussed here related closely to the final paper the students had to submit to the Principles of Economics class and (as the students said) the reading passages discussed in the English class helped to clarify some obscure points that were crucial for their work in the parallel course.

5. Classroom Activities

Activities proposed for each reading attempted to reflect the methodology involved in handling social science texts. Most of them were carried out in Spanish: discussion of concepts, summarizing ideas, transferring information to schematic form, analysis and comment on the data, and extricating the author's opinion. Linguistic activities included handling vocabulary (guessing meaning from word components, finding cognates, using the context) and discovering the ways in which rhetorical functions were indicated. Grammar as such was never a central part of the class. Other activities, spontaneously deriving from the interpretation of the text, were comparing authors' ideas on the basis of the reading and the students' knowledge, discussing concepts as expressed by different authors, contrasting previous knowledge with the fresh input offered by the text, and confronting the content of the readings with the content handled in the Principles of Economics course.

6. Evaluation

Two mid-term examinations, several workshops and a final exam were carried out as part of the assessment procedures. These respond to the general University regulations on examinations. The most important contribution of the students, however, was in the form of individual papers that they presented at the end of the course. This type of exercise had never been tried before with beginning students, since we usually tend to underestimate their capacity in handling the language and making their own decisions. The task consisted of finding a text of their interest, selecting a passage (one or two pages at the most), reading it, and making a summary in Spanish. Each student had to explain orally his choice, the strategies he had used for the interpretation of the text and the use he had made of external aids (dictionary, available translations, etc.) This turned out to be a most valuable exercise. In the final discussion with the students it was possible to determine how different each individual is in his learning processes, and how varied the strategies to approaching a text can be. Some of the students religiously applied the strategies learned in the course; some of them started by translating the text completely into Spanish; some of them used the dictionary for every other word; others started from the known to the unknown; and some were incapable of handling the text without the help of a friend.

At the end of the course, an evaluation questionnaire was given to the students. The questionnaire included questions on three areas of course organization: objectives, content and methodology. Although the results have not yet been completely analysed, preliminary work suggests a mainly positive reaction to the course.

7. General Observations

It is too soon to evaluate results of an approach to course design used for the first time in our Department. However, some general comments can be made at this point:
  ● Language teaching should not be an end in itself but a means towards achieving external communicative goals. Only in this way can we detach ourselves from the narrow language-oriented objectives that are common in our courses and that restrict learners' development.
  ● The more closely we mirror communicative skills in the native language, the more successful we will be in achieving our goals in the foreign

language. Similarities and not differences should be stressed.

- Breaking away from a formalistic approach to language teaching provides fresh motivation to system-weary students going into tertiary education.
- Although I agree with the claim that teaching a language with a purpose is mainly a matter of methodology, of "involving learners in activities which engage the kind of conceptual and procedural routines which characterize their area of study" (Widdowson 1982), I also believe that content provides a vehicle for engaging the learner's participation and increasing his motivation. Familiarity with a given topic will make the student feel that, for once, he is not at a disadvantage in front of the teacher, who traditionally has provided all the answers.

References

BRITISH COUNCIL, *Team Teaching in ESP, ELT Documents 106*, 1980.

BRITISH COUNCIL, *The ESP Teacher: Role, Development and Prospects, ELT Documents 112*, 1981.

HARVEY, A. and SINDERMANN, *A Specialized Course for Students of Economics and Administration*, Departamento de Economia, Universidad de Chile, 1979.

HARVEY, A. and SINDERMANN, *Reading Strategies for Economics and Administration*, Departamento de Economia, Universidad de Chile, 1981.

LOPEZ, G. and CONOVER, N. Determination of foreign language needs in the Universidad del Valle, *ESPUVALE* No. 3, July 1980.

MOORE, J. *et al.*, *Reading and Thinking in English*, Oxford: OUP, 1979.

SINCLAIR, J. 'Language for Specific Purposes', *English Language Research Journal*, University of Birmingham, 1980.

SKEHAN, P. 'The team-teaching of introductory Economics to overseas students' in *ELT Documents 106*, London: The British Council, 1980.

TADROS, A. 'Prediction in Economics Texts', *English Language Research Journal*, University of Birmingham, 1980.

TADROS, A. *Linguistic prediction in Economics texts*, PhD dissertation, University of Birmingham, 1981.

WIDDOWSON, H. G. 'The Ends and Means of ESP', 1982 (mimeo).

Editor's Comment

Although this paper may, at first sight, seem rather remote from the main concerns of this volume (being set within one of the leading Universities in Colombia), reflection will show this not to be so. Like other contributors (Ballard, James, etc) it has much of interest to say about the characteristics of 'disciplinary culture'. More importantly, de Escorcia demonstrates that collaboration between English and subject staff can still be successful in relatively adverse circumstances, thus offering prospects that did not really exist before, given the widely-held belief that team-teaching enterprises are particularly fragile and need a highly supportive environment. One particularly interesting aspect of this account is the positive and collaborative role played by the students themselves — and the achievement of this may well have wider implications.

JMS

V. Testing and Examining

THE ASSOCIATED EXAMINING BOARD'S TEST IN ENGLISH FOR ACADEMIC PURPOSES (TEAP)

CYRIL J. WEIR

Associated Examining Board

Introduction: In Pursuit of the Communicative Paradigm

In the wake of a greater emphasis on communication in language teaching, a similar paradigm shift is apparent in a number of recent approaches to language testing which take as their starting point language in use as against language usage. These approaches are influenced by a sociolinguistic model of communication where the concern is with the abilities and processes at work, as members of the target group attempt to handle the formal and functional dimensions of speech acts relevant to their needs in appropriate situations.

We need to evaluate samples of performance in certain specific contexts of use, created under particular test constraints, for what they can tell us about a candidate's underlying competence. For this purpose it would first seem necessary to develop a framework of categories for descriptions which would help us to identify the activities our target group are involved in, and to construct realistic and representative test tasks corresponding to these. By applying these categories at the *a priori* test task validation stage, we would hope to avoid some of the problems which have arisen in some earlier efforts at communicative testing where no attempt was made to produce explicit specifications of the candidates' projected language needs in the target situation before test task construction took place. Though we would be cautious in claims for the directness of fit possible between test realization and specification, we would argue that this approach enables us to come closer to matching test tasks with appropriate activities in the target behaviour than would be possible using nonempirical approaches.

What follows below is a brief description of how we have attempted to improve the content validity of our tests.

Stage I: Who to Test?

In Stage I of the TEAP project we established the levels, the discipline areas and the institutions where overseas students were enrolling in the further and higher education sectors. On the basis of the information gathered during this stage, we focussed our research on students following courses in the general subject areas of science, engineering, and social business/administrative studies.

Stage II: What to Test?

In Stage II, we sought to ascertain the communicative demands that are made on students following courses in these general discipline areas. Two methods of enquiry were employed to determine the language tasks facing students in a number of different academic contexts.

During 1980, we carried out a series of visits to educational institutions in different sectors of tertiary education. Observations of science, engineering and social science courses were made at the Universities of Exeter, London and Reading, and also at colleges in Farnborough, Bradford, Newbury and Padworth. During these visits, the general language tasks facing students taking part in lectures, seminars and practical classes were recorded, using an observation schedule derived from the *Schools Council Science Teaching Observation Schedule* (Egglestone *et al.*, 1975) and from John Munby's *Communicative Needs Processing Model* (Munby, 1978). The data generated by these exercises provided us with the framework for our second method of enquiry: the questionnaire.

During 1981 we contacted all the university and polytechnic science, engineering and social science departments, and colleges offering General Certificate of Education (GCE) A-Level science, where we knew from earlier research that there were large numbers of overseas students studying, and asked them to assist us in our project. We then asked those who were willing to cooperate to let us have details of the numbers of overseas students for whom English was not the first language in the country of origin, enrolled on specific courses within their departments, together with numbers of the staff who taught them. Questionnaires were then sent to staff and through them to both British and overseas students. Completed questionnaires were received from 940 overseas students, 530 British students and 559 staff in respect of 43 postgraduate courses, 61 undergraduate courses and 39 A-level centres.

The questionnaire enabled us to ask the students to estimate the frequency with which certain events and activities occurred in respect of the total programme of study they were enrolled on; it also provided us with a general estimate of the amount of difficulty various activities and constraints caused them. The staff were asked to give an overall impression of the frequency of occurrence of various activities with particular reference to the courses they taught, on the programme we had specified. They were also asked to estimate the proportion of overseas and British students on these courses, who had encountered difficulty with particular activities or under particular constraints.

In terms of the type of question that we were able to ask in the questionnaire, reading and writing differ from listening and speaking in that it was easier to ask a more complete set of frequency questions about the former because they are relatively free of the performance constraints that affect the latter grouping. Although we were able to collect data in respect of the level of difficulty these activities and constraints caused in listening and speaking, for various reasons it was often not possible to collect data on the frequency with which the constraints and the activities occurred.

For this reason there are far more blanks in the frequency sections of the summary tables in Appendix I below, when we deal with the constraints and activities involved in listening and speaking in the academic context.

In Appendix I we have summarized the questionnaire returns concerning the frequency with which students had to carry out various communicative activities in the academic context, together with details of the relative levels of difficulty encountered by overseas students as compared to their British counterparts in coping with these tasks and attendant performance constraints. Taking this frequency data separately or, where possible, in conjunction with the difficulty data, we have tried to establish what might be considered as 'key' activities and constraints across levels and disciplines. As most tests can only sample a limited part of the possible domain, it seemed prudent to ensure that we included in the battery those tasks which were common and frequent across disciplines and levels and/or seemed, from the available evidence, more likely to cause problems for the overseas as against the British students.

For example, if we take Table 2, where the major focus is on reading activities, the most frequent activity students have to perform is 'search reading to get information specifically required for assignments'. Compare this with 'reading critically to establish and evaluate the author's position on a particular topic' which, though it is marginally more important in terms of the relative amount of difficulty it causes overseas as against British students, in fact it is only the social science student who really has to cope with this task to any great extent. It would seem prudent, in taking decisions about what reading tasks to include in a time-constrained, communicative, proficiency test, to have this kind of information available.

Stage III: How to Test?

During the third stage of the project, which is scheduled to continue until August 1983, we are concerned with designing and validating a variety of test formats to establish the best methods for assessing a student's performance level on those tasks and under those constraints that the research to date has indicated to be important to overseas students following academic courses through the medium of English.

We have included as Appendix II below the copies of the introductions the students were given for each Session of the pilot version of TEAP. These will give the reader an indication of the nature of the test activities that we are concerned with. It is envisaged that all students would take Session I, where the components are related topically through a theme selected from popular science. Students would then take the version of Session II most appropriate to the discipline area in which they are going to study. There will also be a Session III for assessing the student's spoken ability, which we hope will be ready early in 1983.

Appendix I: Summary of Difficulty and Frequency Data from Stage II: What to Test?

KEY

(A) DIFFICULTY

Col. 1 OS
Difficulties encountered by overseas students ranked according to total percentages of those experiencing 'some' or 'a lot' of difficulty with certain activities and performance constraints.

Col. 2 OS-BR
Rank ordering according to percentage differences between overseas and British students encountering 'some' or 'a lot' of difficulty with certain activities and performance constraints.

Col. 3 Staff OS
Staff estimates of the proportions ('a lot' or 'some') of the overseas students experiencing difficulty with certain activities and performance constraints, ranked in order of magnitude.

Col. 4 Staff OS-BR
Percentage differences in staff estimates of proportions ('a lot' or 'some') of the British and overseas students experiencing difficulty with certain activities and performance constraints, ranked in order of magnitude.

Col. 5 Staff Impt.
Staff estimates (where available) of the importance of a particular criterion ranked according to the percentage totals for 'high' and 'medium' importance.

(B) FREQUENCY

×	20–39%	of overseas students
× ×	40–59%	'never' having to do the task

+	20–39%	
+ +	40–59%	of overseas students
+⁺+	60–79%	'often' having to do the task
‡ ‡	80–100%	

OS	= overseas students	Eng.	= Engineering
BR	= British students	Sci.	= Science
H	= high	S.Sci.	= Social Science
M	= medium	U	= undergraduate
N	= never	P	= postgraduate
O	= often	A	= A-level GCE

(A) DIFFICULTY

	Col. 1 OS	Col. 2 OS-BR	Col. 3 Staff OS	Col. 4 Staff OS-BR
(1) Teachers and other students talk very fast	55.0% (2)	35.7%	—	—
(2) Their accents or pronunciation are different from what they are used to	52.7% (3)	27.6%	—	—
(3) Writing down quickly and clearly all the notes they want to	41.5% (10)	8.9%	—	—
(4) More than one person is speaking as in group discussion	41.1% (4)	26.4%	—	—
(5) Understanding informal language	38.6% (1)	36.9% (3)	52.5% (1)	47.5%
(6) Thinking of and using suitable abbreviations	33.9% (7)	21.7%	—	—
(7) Understanding spoken description or narrative	31.0% (5")	26.3% (2)	53.2% (2)	41.9%

(B) FREQUENCY (Based on highest returns (N and O for all classes)

Eng. U	Eng. P	Sci. U	Sci. P	Sci. A	S.Sci. U	S.Sci. P
N O	N O	N O	N O	N O	N O	N O

(8)	Recognizing individual words in what is being said	30.8% (6)	26.3%	—	—			
(9)	People speak quietly	29.3% (13)	2.3%	—	—			
(10)	Recognizing what is important and worth noting	28.0% (12)	5.8%	—	—			
(11)	Understanding completely what the speaker is saying and linking this to what he has said earlier	23.6% (9)	12.9%	—	—			
(12)	Understanding spoken instructions	21.1% (8)	19.0% (4)	44.1% (3)	35.3%	×	+	$^{++}$ $^{++}$
(13)	Organizing the notes they take down so that they can understand them when they read them later	18.2% (15)	−0.8%	—				
(14)	Understanding the subject matter of the talk	18.1% (14)	0.6% (1)	66.2% (5)	11.4%			
(15)	Recognizing where sentences end and begin	9.9% (11)	7.8%	—				
	Making notes	—	(5)	40.2% (4)	17.6%	××	++	‡‡

Table 1. *Listening*

	(A) DIFFICULTY		(B) FREQUENCY							
	Col. 1 OS	Col. 2 OS-BR	Eng. U	Eng. P	Sci. U	Sci. P	Sci. A	S.Sci. A	S.Sci. U	S.Sci. P
			N	O	N	O	N	O	N	O
Reading texts where the subject matter is very complicated	(1) 67.9	(7) 8.4								
Critical reading to establish and evaluate the author's position on a particular topic	(2) 55.3	(2) 21.8	××	×	××	×	××	+		++
Reading quickly to find out how useful it would be to study a particular text more intensively	(3) 49.7	(1) 26.2	×	+	×	+	×	+	+	++
Search reading to get information specifically required for assignments	(4) 39.6	(3) 18.3	++	++	++	++	+	++	‡‡	++
Reading carefully to understand all the information in a text:	(5) 35.0	(6) 8.5								
• duplicated notes			++	++	++	++	+	++	++	++
• questions done in class or for homework			++	++	++	++	++	++	++	+
• laboratory worksheets			++	×	+	+	×	××	××	+
• examination questions			++	++	+	+	++	++	+	++
• textbooks, whole or part			+	++	++	++	++	+	++	++
Making notes from textbooks	(6) 25.9	(5) 12.7	×	+	+	+	+	+	++	++
Reading to get the main information from a text	(7) 25.8	(4) 14.3	+	+	++	++	+	++	++	++

Table 2. *Reading*

(A) *DIFFICULTY*

	Col. 1 OS	Col. 2 OS-BR	Col. 3 Staff OS	Col. 4 Staff OS-BR	Col. 5 Staff Impt.
Using a wide and varied range of vocabulary	(1) 61.9	(1) 41.2	(5) 66.9	(3) 30.1	(10) 41.3
Using a variety of grammatical structures	(2) 47.2	(3) 30.7	(4) 70.0	(5) 17.7	(12) 22.2
Using appropriate vocabulary	(3) 46.4	(2) 34.2	(7) 63.8	(1) 33.2	(4) 69.6
Expressing what you want to say clearly	(4) 40.8	(7) 14.5	(3) 70.2	(4) 21.5	(2) 90.9
Using appropriate grammatical structures	(5) 40.4	(4) 24.8	(2) 71.4	(2) 30.6	(8) 43.3
Arranging and developing written work	(6) 35.8	(8) 13.7	(6) 65.5	(9) 10.3	(3) 82.1
Writing grammatically correct sentences	(7) 33.5	(5) 20.7	(1) 75.3	(6) 16.3	(6) 46.9
The subject matter	(8) 29.9	(6) 18.8	(9) 60.6	(10) 10.2	(1) 91.8
Spelling	(9) 24.3	(10) 2.0	(8) 62.1	(8) 11.3	(9) 42.3
Punctuation	(10) 21.4	(9) 8.9	(10) 59.6	(7) 12.9	(11) 39.3
Tidiness	(11) 16.8	(12) − 5.3	(12) 47.1	(12) − 4.3	(5) 62.8
Handwriting	(12) 14.2	(11) − 4.1	(11) 49.4	(11) − 2.3	(7) 44.6

(B) *FREQUENCY*

		Eng. U		Eng. P		Sci. U		Sci. P		Sci. A		S.Sci. U		S.Sci. P	
		N	O	N	O	N	O	N	O	N	O	N	O	N	O
more than a paragraph in	coursework	+	+	+	+	+	+		+	+	+		+	×	+
	examinations	+	+	+	+	+	+		+	+	+			×	+
about a paragraph in	coursework		+		+		+				+		+	××	+
	examinations		+		+	×	+		+			×	+		
less than a paragraph in	coursework		+		+	×	+		+		+	+	+	+	+
	examinations		+	+	+	×	+	×	+		+		+	+̟	+

Table 3. *Writing*

(A) DIFFICULTY

(B) FREQUENCY (Based on highest returns for seminars and practical classes)

	Col. 1 OS	Col. 2 OS-BR	Col. 3 Staff OS	Col. 4 Staff OS-BR	Eng. U		Eng. P		Sci. U		Sci. P		Sci. A		S.Sci. U		S.Sci. P	
					N	O	N	O	N	O	N	O	N	O	N	O	N	O
Giving oral reports or short talks	(1) 50.3	(1) 38.4	(7)† 39.9	(10)† 12.3	×	×	×		×	×	×	×	×	×			+	
Expressing counter-arguments to points raised by teachers in discussions	(2) 48.1	(4) 26.6	(3) 54.4	(6) 17.9														
Explaining your opinions when they are not immediately understood in discussions	(3) 45.9	(3) 27.7	(2) 55.3	(3) 23.8														
Expressing counter-arguments to points raised by other students in discussions	(4) 45.0	(2) 29.8	(5)† 47.8	(7)† 17.2														

Expressing your own opinions in discussions	(5) 37.2	(4) 26.7	(4) 50.6	(1) 25.2	×	+ +	+ +	+ +	+	+ +	+ +	+ +	+ +
Answering questions asked by teachers	(6) 31.6	(6) 20.9	(1) 63.2	(5) 19.6	+ +	+ +	+ +	+	+ +	+ +	+ +	+ +	+ +
Asking teachers questions	(7) 22.0	(7) 17.5	(6) 46.8	(4) 23.3	+ +	+ +	+	+ +	+ +	+ +	+ +	+	+
Answering questions asked by other students	(8) 19.3	(9) 12.7	(8)† 31.0	(8)† 12.8									
Working with other students using English to communicate	(9) 18.7	(8) 16.4	(9) 30.8	(2) 24.0	‡ ‡	+ +	+ +	+ +	+ +	+ +	+ +	+ +	+ +
Asking other students questions	(10) 14.5	(10) 11.8	(10)† 23.3	(9)† 12.4									
Actively taking part in discussions					+	+	+	+	+	+	+ +	+ +	+ +

† High proportion of 'don't know'.

Table 1. *Speaking*

Appendix II

(A) General Introduction to Session I of Pilot Version of TEAP

Session I of the test has four parts. You must write all your answers in this booklet. Here is a brief description of the four parts of the test so that you know what to expect. There will be detailed instructions before each part.

PART ONE

This is a test of your ability to read in English and to write in English about what you have read. You have **2 tasks** to do in 75 minutes.

Task One — You have to write a summary of parts of a passage. To help you to do this you should make brief notes while reading the passage.

Task Two — You have to write short answers to a number of questions on the same passage.

PART TWO

This is a test of your ability to understand spoken English. You have **one task** to do in approximately 10 minutes.

You will hear a short tape recording ONCE only. During pauses in the recording, you have to write down, in the space provided in this booklet, what the speaker has said.

PART THREE

This is another test of your ability to understand spoken English. You have to make notes and use them to answer a number of questions. You have **2 tasks** to do in approximately 50 minutes.

Task One — You will hear a tape recording of a short lecture ONCE only. A written OUTLINE of the main points of the lecture is printed in this booklet to help you to follow what the speaker is saying. This LECTURE OUTLINE consists of three important statements from the passage, each followed by questions. While listening to the lecture you have to make NOTES in the spaces provided as after the lecture you will have time to go through these NOTES and use them to write ANSWERS.

Task Two — You have to write a summary of parts of the lecture using the LECTURE OUTLINE and your NOTES and ANSWERS.

PART FOUR

This is a test of your knowledge of English grammar. It consists of 60 multiple choice questions. You have 30 minutes to complete this final task of Session I.

(B) General Introduction to Session II of Pilot Version of TEAP

Session II of the test has three parts. You must write all your answers in this booklet. Here is a brief description of the three parts of the test, so that you know what to expect. There will be detailed instructions before each part.

PART ONE

This is a test of your ability to read in English. There are 3 different reading passages. You have **3 tasks** to do in 80 minutes.

Task One — Answering multiple choice questions on the first reading passage.

Task Two — Finding words missing from a second passage and writing these words in boxes provided.

Task Three — Writing short answers to a number of questions on a third passage.

PART TWO

This is a test of your ability to understand spoken English by making notes and using them to answer questions. You will have only **one task** to do in approximately 30 minutes.

You will hear a tape recording of a short interview ONCE only. A written OUTLINE of the interview is printed in this booklet to help you to follow what the speakers are saying. The OUTLINE consists of a number of QUESTIONS. You have to make NOTES in the spaces provided while you are listening to the interview. After the interview, you will have time to go through the NOTES you have made and use them to write ANSWERS.

PART THREE

This is a test of your ability to write in English, in complete sentences, and organize your work so that what you write is clear and answers the questions you are asked. You have **2 tasks** to do in 65 minutes.

Task One — Writing a summary using:
a) notes made on the third reading passage in Part One.
b) relevant information from Part Two.

Task Two — Rewriting a short passage which contains a number of errors, making all the necessary corrections.

References

EGGLESTONE, J. F. *et al. A Science Teaching Observation Schedule* (Schools Council Research Studies), London: Macmillan, 1975.
MUNBY, J. *Communicative Syllabus Design*, Cambridge: Cambridge University Press, 1978.

Editor's Comment

What is particularly impressive about Cyril Weir's account of the AEB's Test in English for Academic Purposes is the considerable amount of time invested in validating test content, particularly at the *a priori* stage. This has clearly involved developing more systematic procedures for test task construction than might have been employed in the past. It is particularly encouraging to EFL practitioners to see the openness with which AEB are approaching this large task — an openness that compares favourably with the design and validation of similar tests in recent years.

RCW

'NAVIGATION TECHNIQUES' FOR 16+ VOCATIONAL STUDENTS: ASSESSMENT PROCEDURES AND LANGUAGE SKILLS DEVELOPMENT[1]

PHYLLIS SANTAMARIA GOVE

University of Exeter

Introduction

The riots of the summer of 1981 in Britain have produced more action on youth unemployment than years of rational argument. Recent unemployment figures suggesting that 60 per cent of 16 to 18 year olds will soon be unemployed (*Times Educational Supplement* 6.11.1981) have been rapidly followed by proposals to remedy the situation.

In fact, the Government has already begun creating the New Training Initiative (NTI) with a one billion pound budget, and the House of Lords Select Committee on Employment has recommended a two billion pound package to cut unemployment by a million over the next two to three years (*Times Educational Supplement* 18.6.1982). Both proposals have the extension of education and training at the top of their lists, emphasizing that the new measures should be directed mainly at the under-18s.

These training proposals are focussing attention on school leavers who have either not obtained sufficient 16+ examination results to continue with academic courses, not secured one of the increasingly scarce apprenticeships, or not decided which vocational skills to train for. In dealing with this new training clientele, it has generally been found that 16+ examination results are neither available nor relevant to the demands of vocational courses, and that the nature of vocational training and work itself has been changing.

The traditional pattern of industrially-based apprenticeships with day-release courses in Further Education (FE) colleges leading to life-long held jobs is rapidly giving way to a new pattern of general vocational training. Initial full-time general courses, which may include some work experience,

[1]The on-going project referred to in this paper is known as the Exeter Vocational Training Language Study, and is sponsored by the Social Science Research Council.

introduce trainees to a vocational skill area as a basis for specialization when jobs occur.

This new pattern of training and employment demanding a more skilled yet adaptable and flexible workforce requires a reappraisal of the type of training offered. The central issues emerging from the many proposals currently being devised are as follows:

1) the development of innovative assessment procedures which provide diagnostic information to teacher and student about the student's abilities and needs for development in the 'key skills' of language, numeracy, problem-solving and practical work

2) the maximum development of students' 'key skills' in the contexts provided throughout training or across the curriculum

In the light of these central issues, the objectives of the Exeter Vocational Training Language Study (hereafter known as the Exeter Study) are to characterize vocational engineering students' language skill levels upon course entry, and to analyse language use in the first year of full-time technician and craft level vocational engineering courses. The study originated from a request by an Inner London Education Authority (ILEA) Language and Literacy Unit working party of FE lecturers for a language-needs analysis of vocational courses popular with English as a Second Language (ESL) speakers. ESL and communication lecturers would like systematized information about the language and study skills needed for mainstream vocational courses, to determine whether their assumptions about communication needs for subject-specific areas are valid.

Preliminary observations and interviews have revealed that not only ESL but also first language (L1) speakers experience difficulties with language skills on vocational courses. Therefore, ESL speakers' problems and needs are considered as occupying part of a continuum of language needs for all students on vocational courses.

1. Current Developments in Communicative Assessment Procedures

Before discussing the proposed assessment procedures to be used in this study, it is worthwhile summarizing the two mainstreams of communicative assessment procedures: communicative testing in EFL, and profiling and reviewing schemes of 'key skills' for L1 16+ vocational students and trainees.

Some of the common features shared by both assessment procedures are as follows:

1) Assessment design is based on a needs analysis of the skills required to perform a task or job.

2) Authentic materials and/or settings are employed as the context for assessment.

3) Results are reported in terms of behavioural criteria, providing more information to the assessment consumer upon which to base a selection decision, than the results of norm-referenced tests or school-leaving examinations.

The following two sections summarize the differing approaches in L2 communicative testing and in L1 profiling and reviewing schemes for 16 + vocational students.

2. Communicative Testing in EFL

Communicative tests of English for Academic Purposes (EAP) are typified by the British Council's English Language Testing Service (ELTS), and the Associated Examining Board (AEB)'s Test in English for Academic Purposes (this volume). The following description of a language needs analysis and test content specification for English for A-level science recently undertaken (Gove, 1981) will serve to illustrate the methods used and the pragmatic considerations for test design. The students being considered were overseas students who had come to Britain for their studies, and British students sharing the A-level courses, who provided data for comparison.

Figure 1, 'Language and Study Skills Needs Analysis', presents the main components which determine test content:

1. *Data for Analysis*

   (a) *Specification of Communicative Language Needs*
   Munby's (1978) categories provide a descriptive framework for communicative language needs. The observation schedule devised by a Schools Council project on science teaching (Eggleston *et al.*, 1975) and amended by Cyril Weir of the AEB provides a guide for recording the linguistic transactions in lessons, as well as students' uses of texts for reference and the types of written work demanded by a course.

   (b) *Student and Staff Questionnaires*
   The questionnaires devised by Cyril Weir detail the frequency of occurrence and levels of difficulty encountered by students in the language and study skills areas. These results serve as student and staff observations to be compared with the results of lesson observations and interviews.

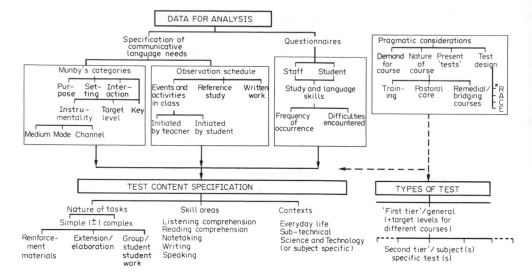

*R: Relevance = 1   Do the tests reflect the specifications identified in the needs analysis?
          = 2   Is test information able to guide decisions about the candidate?
A: Acceptability = Will the users of the test accept its content and format?
C: Comparability = Can the test scores obtained at different times and from different groups
                     be compared?
E: Economy   = Do the tests provide as much information as required with minimum
                     expenditure of time, effort and resources? (Carroll, 1980:13)

Figure 1. *Language and Study Skills Needs Analysis*

2. *Test Content Specification* (see Figure 2: 'Test Content Specification
Model')

Data results indicate the relevant course language and study skills to be
tested as combinations of the following descriptive categories:

(a) *Nature of Tasks*
   1. *Simple/Complex* depending on either or both:
      (a) *Size*: "physical extent of the text (oral or graphic) being
          produced or comprehended"
      (b) *Complexity*: "the extent to which the focuses of a text
          multiply in regard to topics, styles or presentation and
          semantic fields" (Carroll, 1980:31)
   2. *Reinforcement materials*: visual display in the form of
      demonstrations, specimens or other 'realia'; accompanying text,
      graphs, diagrams, etc. which help to disambiguate oral or
      graphic text for the learner
   3. *Extension, elaboration*: the opportunity for the learner to have
      the text repeated by clarification in an interactive situation, or
      by being able to read a text in his/her own time or by reference
      to dictionaries, supplementary texts, etc.

4. *Group*: Group or student-student interaction involving the opportunity to 'talk' about a topic or work being done as a means of expanding meaning for the learner

(b) *Skill Areas* to be tested include

1. Listening comprehension
2. Reading comprehension
3. Notetaking
4. Writing
5. Speaking

(c) *Contexts* for testing are drawn from

1. Everyday life

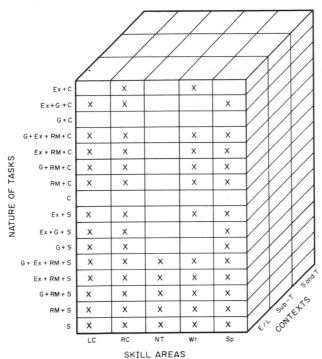

NATURE OF TASKS	LC	RC	NT	Wr	Sp
Ex + C		X		X	
Ex + G + C	X	X			X
G + C					
G + Ex + RM + C	X	X		X	X
Ex + RM + C	X	X		X	X
G + RM + C	X	X		X	X
RM + C	X	X		X	X
C					
Ex + S	X	X		X	X
Ex + G + S	X	X			X
G + S	X	X			X
G + Ex + RM + S	X	X	X	X	X
Ex + RM + S	X	X	X	X	X
G + RM + S	X	X	X	X	X
RM + S	X	X	X	X	X
S	X	X	X	X	X

SKILL AREAS

SKILL AREAS
LC: Listening comprehension
RC: Reading comprehension
NT: Notetaking
Wr: Writing
Sp: Speaking

NATURE OF TASKS
S: Simple
C: Complex
RM: Reinforcement materials
Ex: Extension, elaboration
G: Group

CONTEXTS
E/L: Everyday life
Sub-T: Sub-technical
S&T: Science and technology

Figure 2. *Test Content Specification Model*

    2. Sub-technical areas

    3. Subject-specific areas of science and technology

3. *Pragmatic Considerations*
Factors which greatly affect test design are:

(a) *Demand* for the course

(b) *Nature* of the course: provisions for practical components in the course, pastoral care, remedial or bridging courses

(c) *Present tests*: effectiveness, other subject-specific examination prerequisites such as O-level science

(d) *Test design*: The features of relevance, acceptability, comparability and economy (Carroll, 1980:13) are also to be incorporated into test design.

4. *Types of Test*
The degree of specification demanded by the test will determine whether a 'first tier' or general test will suffice or whether 'second tier' or subject-specific tests will also be required.

This needs analysis of A-level science specified test content areas, but certain pragmatic considerations determined that it was not necessary to devise a communicative college entrance test for A-level science students. These considerations included the low demand for courses due to the high fees for overseas students, the academic pre-requisites of O-level science or equivalent, the nature of the A-level course, and the success of existing testing and interview systems at both colleges surveyed.

3. Profiling and Reviewing Schemes for 16+ Vocational Students

Returning to the needs of the L1 16+ applicant to a full-time vocational course in an FE college or MSC (Manpower Services Commission) scheme, we find that there are different pragmatic considerations to those outlined above for overseas applicants to A-level science. Some of these considerations are as follows:

1. There is a wider clientele for FE and training courses than has previously been the case, because of the development of schemes such as the 'New Training Initiative', a government-sponsored full-time vocational training scheme for 16 to 18 year olds. The NTI is run by the MSC.

2. There is fierce competition for fewer apprenticeships in all vocational areas.

3. Although nearly 90 per cent of school leavers are now getting one graded O-level or CSE, college tutors interviewed have found that unless pupils get CSE Grade 3 or better in English and Maths, they cannot cope with the demands of some vocational courses.

4. Some applicants to college and training schemes have had careers advice but are not certain about their career choices.

5. Other applicants have had little careers advice and therefore need initial career guidance from the college or MSC scheme.

6. Communications tutors in some ILEA colleges are developing 'foundation courses' for ESL and L1 speakers to develop their language and study skills — 'navigation techniques' — to prepare them for mainstream courses.

Several research projects have been undertaken in response to these considerations in order to provide information about 'key skills' training, with special reference to the less-qualified school leaver. The following synopses of the projects will give an indication of their fields of research:

1. The 'Young People Starting Work' project has developed the Job Components Inventory as a basis for improving the job prospects of less-qualified school leavers. 450 jobs held by 1,000 young people have been analysed to determine which 'key skills' are required in the following categories: use of tools and equipment, perceptual and physical, mathematical, communication, and decision-making and responsibility. The skills information is then applied to problems in curriculum, careers guidance and training design (Banks *et al.*, 1981).

2. The MSC 'Grouping of Skills' project has developed the Basic Skills Checklist and Matrix for "use as a simple and quick analytical tool with which to examine any job or training activity". The information provides a guide for making decisions about products, activities, and experiences best suited to trainee abilities. In addition, profiles of trainees are devised to report on progress during training and to provide information on skill accomplishments as a form of credentials (Freshwater, 1981 and 1982).

3. The 'Trainee-centred Reviewing' project has developed a system of recording and reviewing schemes for trainees in MSC programmes similar to personal record systems in use in education and industry. Trainees participate in the reviewing process by identifying and negotiating training objectives with the trainer, and maintaining a recording system during training. Trainees are encouraged to acquire or develop 'self-interviewing' skills for use on or after training (Pearce *et al.*, 1982).

4. The ILEA Further and Higher Education Curriculum Development Project (1982) has devised single subject (numeracy, communication and science) and whole course profiling schemes. Profiling is a "process through which one can provide objective evidence of what a student *can* do . . . through detailed performance checklisting". Both student and tutor participate in the process of monitoring the progress of the student.

4. Analysis of Language Use across the Curriculum

In the Exeter Study, a sample of vocational engineering students at a Devon and a London college will be observed throughout an academic year. Their language skill levels will be rated using conventional norm-referenced test (NFER Senior English test for vocational students), and a pilot pre-testing of the British Council's ELTS non-academic module communicative test for L2 speakers. Experiments will also be conducted as to the feasibility of using lecturer-ratings of language skill levels according to a behavioural checklist as used in the various profiling and reviewing schemes outlined above. Student self-assessments of their language skill levels will be piloted, and the students' school-leaving examination results will also be recorded.

It is hoped that several basic questions will be answered by these variables in relation to the analysis of language skills used on the courses. First of all, is it possible to specify the language skills levels that students should have upon course entry? Secondly, what is the most effective means of determining what these language skill levels are? Thirdly, will these assessment procedures provide diagnostic information to be used not only by communication but also subject-specific lecturers to develop students' language skills throughout the year?

The main focus of the Exeter Study is to provide an analysis of language use throughout the subject-specific areas in vocational engineering, with a view to determining core language skills and functions. In the process of research for the needs analysis of A-level science, my attention was drawn to the similarity of concern with scientific processes by various writers in the fields of science education for native speakers, and English for science and technology for second-language speakers. Clive Carré's (1981) work on the role of language in science for native speaker learners illustrates the necessity of pupils' being exposed to and utilizing all language skill areas in the development of concepts and knowledge of process in science. Full-time vocational engineering courses provide the opportunity, often for the first time, for the less academically-oriented student to develop an understanding of processes through practical 'hands on' experience. It is possible that the combination of practical and theoretical work provided in these courses contributes to what several technical lecturers have characterized in interviews as the students' 'coming on' or 'blossoming' substantially in their first year in a vocational course.

The work of Selinker, Trimble and Trimble (1976) provides a description of rhetorical functions and techniques in science and technology which incorporate scientific processes. A working model for developing communicative competence in ESL speakers has been devised by McAllister and Robson (1981) utilizing communicative functions similar to those outlined by Selinker, Trimble and Trimble as rhetorical functions and techniques. Finally, the work done by the Assessment of Performance Unit (APU) of the Department of Education and Science (1978) on science in

British schools clearly exploits the idea of science processes in order to assess science performance.

In analysing language use across the curriculum it seems evident that an investigation of how rhetorical functions and techniques are developed in subject-specific areas is required. As technician and craft level engineers need to specialize and re-specialize throughout their working lives, it is even more imperative that their language skills, and especially those required for reading technical manuals, are more highly developed.

5. Conclusion

A review of the pragmatic considerations outlined suggests that suitable diagnostic assessment procedures must be explored and developed for the new clientele of FE colleges and training schemes. These should identify the needs of mainstream vocational courses, provide a language profile report which states in behavioural terms how able a student is to meet course demands, and suggest syllabus components for foundation or supplementary work. Unless such steps are taken, many will flounder in courses (and later jobs) with language needs beyond them, leaving them unable to cope.

The current economic situation is forcing educational and training establishments to accommodate more students of the 16 to 18 age range who have previously been ignored or excluded because of lack of suitable qualifications, or because unskilled job opportunities were available. Language assessment in the initial stage of a course or as part of a continuous monitoring of progress, when based upon needs analyses of specific courses or jobs, can serve to develop 'navigation techniques' for both first and second language speakers of English.

References

BANKS, M. H., JACKSON, P., STAFFORD, E. and WARR, P. 'Young people starting work', MSC Chief Training Adviser's Branch, Moorfoot, Sheffield SI 4PQ, 1981 (mimeo).
CARRÉ, C. *Science* (Language Teaching and Learning Series), Ward Lock Educational, 1981.
CARROLL, B. J. *Testing Communicative Performance—An Interim Study*, Oxford: Pergamon, 1980.
DEPARTMENT OF EDUCATION AND SCIENCE (Assessment of Performance Unit) *Science Progress Report 1977-78*, DES, 1978.
EGGLESTONE, J. F., GALTON, J. J. and JONES, M. E. *A Science Teaching Observation Schedule*, Macmillan Education/Schools Council Research Studies, 1975.
FRESHWATER, M. *Basic Skills Checklist and Matrix*, MSC Training Services, Moorfoot, Sheffield, 1981.
FRESHWATER, M. *The Basic Skills Analysis: how a checklist can help to make the most of training opportunities*, MSC Training Services, Moorfoot, Sheffield, 1982.
GOVE, P. S. 'Aspects of communicative testing with special reference to English for science and mathematics 'A' level', Unpublished MA dissertation, University of Exeter, 1981.
ILEA/FHE CURRICULUM DEVELOPMENT PROJECT, 'RSA/ILEA continuous assessment and profile certificate scheme', Westminster College (Room 273), Battersea Park Road, London SW11 2JR, 1982 (mimeo).

McALLISTER, J. and ROBSON, M. 'Studying in a second language: a programme for developing communicative competence', Shipley College, Yorkshire, 1981 (mimeo).

MUNBY, J. *Communicative Syllabus Design*, Cambridge: CUP, 1978.

PEARCE, B., VARNEY, E., FLEGG, D. and WALDMAN, P. 'Trainee-Centred Reviewing: helping trainees to help themselves', MSC Special Programmes, Selkirk House, 166 High Holborn, London W1V 6PF, 1982.

SELINKER, L., TRIMBLE, M. R. TODD and TRIMBLE, L. 'Presuppositional rhetorical information in EST discourse', *TESOL Quarterly* **10**, 1976.

Editor's Comment

Phyllis Gove pinpoints the important role that training in language and communication skills has to play in the rapidly-shifting 16–18 year old (un)employment field in today's Britain. Clearly, the new pattern of general vocational training (and subsequent retraining) must include teaching the relevant communicative activities that are an integral part of the student's vocational course. This in turn requires communicative assessment procedures of the type outlined in this paper. A particularly interesting section of Phyllis Gove's paper relates to part of the Exeter Study using, in an L1 situation, a communicative test designed initially for L2 students, viz. the British Council's non-academic module—proof indeed of sizeable commonality between the L1 and L2 testing/teaching fields.

RCW

TESTING COMMUNICATION STUDIES AT A-LEVEL

DAVID NEILL

Exeter College

Introduction

In the teaching of English in higher education outside the UK, it has been recognised for several years that students need to be trained in the use of particular varieties of English. Consequently the field of English for Academic Purposes (EAP) is now a fairly well-established branch of teaching English as a Foreign Language (EFL). In contrast, one of the main points to emerge from the 'Communication in English' conference at the University of Aston in Birmingham in 1982 was that in higher education in Britain there is also a great need to improve the communication skills of students, and that with some exceptions very little has been done so far. However, in recent years A-level Communication Studies has been developed, which students can take in the last two years of school or at college of further education before going on to higher education or taking up employment. This may go some way towards improving the situation.

Before outlining the content of Communication Studies A-level and the manner in which it is assessed, I shall examine the influences that have led to changes in English teaching overseas and in the UK and draw parallels between them to partly explain the birth of the new A-level.

1. Developments in English at Home and Abroad

There has been considerable concern in recent years about the teaching of English language to native speakers at all levels. The classical tradition in the British educational system and the 'two cultures' view of either arts *or* sciences has meant, particularly at advanced levels, that English language teaching has been based around the study of English literature. The critical essay seems to have been the main aim, and novels and poetry have been the staple diet of English language students. Language and literature have been (and still are) intertwined, a situation perpetuated by examination board syllabuses.

This was equally true of the EFL (English as a Foreign Language) world up to the 1960s. Books written for teaching English in Africa included most of the 'greats' of English literature, such as Shakespeare, in their lists of recommended textbooks for school libraries. English Language books gave advice on the judicious use of sellotape in preserving such scarce English language teaching material, and conjured up a picture of pioneering English teachers under arduous circumstances bravely taking 'civilization' to the darker corners of the world. Much of the developing world began to see such language teaching as 'cultural imperialism', and this in turn partly accounted for the birth of the ESP (English for Specific Purposes) movement.

In Britain, as greater numbers of native speakers stayed on for further and higher education, it was gradually felt that English language teaching based around English literature was in some way inappropriate to the needs of the students. This questioning of English teaching seems to have occurred later in England than abroad, for equally pioneering teachers were still using novels as the basis of their language teaching in Liberal Studies classes for students on vocational technical college courses in Britain up to the late 1970s. Clearly their intention was twofold: as well as the overt aim of improving students' reading skills and command of written English, there was an additional underlying intention of cultural enrichment.

When the reaction came, it was extreme. In the early 1970s, courses for native speakers were developed, similar to ESP courses for overseas students, by such bodies as the Business Education Council (BEC) and the Technician Education Council (TEC). Syllabuses were developed which confined students to activities such as writing business letters and technical reports, reading memos and instruction manuals. For the supposedly more academic students following full-time A-level courses, the Associated Examining Board introduced in 1976 the Communication Studies syllabus, which may represent the pendulum swinging back from the extreme 'job specific' view of language teaching which has prevailed in recent years. For the course is not intended to prepare students for the language of a particular job, but rather to make the student aware of the varieties of language used in commerce, industry and elsewhere, and to produce language appropriate to a particular situation, whatever that happens to be. The Associated Examining Board (AEB) defines Communication Studies as "a study of the arts, practices and media of communication, including formulating, gathering, receiving and interpretation of ideas, information and attitudes".

For the purposes of this paper I shall outline the methods used for testing Communication Studies at A-level, and in so doing shall describe the contents of the course.

2. AEB Communication Studies Examination—an Overview

The assessment consists of:

- Paper 1 — a written paper of four essays on communications topics (40%)
- Paper 2 — a use-of-English examination (30%)
- A project on a topic of the student's choice (20%)

● An oral examination, based around the student's project (10%)

3. Written Paper 1

This is an examination of a fairly traditional kind in which students are required to write four essay answers in three hours. The paper is divided into four sections:

● development of communications (3.1)
● theory of communication (3.2)
● mass communications (3.3)
● means of communication (3.4)

Typical questions from each section are given below.

3.1 Development of Communications

"Take any one of the systems and innovations that led to the great increase in communication in this country in the 19th century and describe its particular contribution."

3.2 Theory of Communication

"Analyse a communication situation of your choice in terms of *two* communication models, including at least one of the following: Berlo, Barnlund, Shannon and Weaver, Schramm."

3.3 Mass Communications

"A 'gatekeeper' is an accepted description of a person who can determine if and how a message is transmitted. Illustrate, with examples, any aspects of the concept of 'gatekeeping' in the mass media."

3.4 Means of Communication

"Analyse the networks of communication in any large institution with which you are familiar. Illustrate your answer with a chart or charts."

3.5 Comment on Paper 1

There are three points worth mentioning in relation to Paper 1.

3.51. As with all human knowledge, the compartmentalization of the paper into four sections involves the creation of artificial divisions, and this is recognized by the examiners. Consequently the examiners may place a question on a particular topic in any of the four sections. For example, the communication of policies by political parties is one topic included in the syllabus. A student may be asked in the 'Development' section to outline changes that have occurred since the industrial revolution in the strategies adopted by political parties to publicise their policies. Alternatively the student may be asked in the 'Theory' section to, say, apply communication models to a party political broadcast. Another possibility would be for the topic to appear in the 'Mass Communications' section, where the student could be asked to assess the impact of the mass media on the strategies adopted by political parties. Finally the examinee might be required in the 'Means of Communication' section to outline the principles on which he would organize a local election campaign, and to state how these principles might be put into practice.

Whereas this compartmentalization may be academically sound, it makes considerable demands on the student, who has to think on his feet during the three hours of the exam, and to recognize the connections between seemingly discrete areas of knowledge. It significantly reduces the utility of any rote learning to the student, and this can only be a step in the right direction educationally. It may, however, be unreasonably difficult for an A-level student to do, bearing in mind his general academic level and degree of intellectual development. It has certainly not been unreasonably difficult up to now.

3.52. A second point worth noting concerns the section of Paper 1 entitled 'Development of Communications'. This section seems to many teachers to be concerned with a different area of academic enquiry in comparison to the other three sections of Paper 1. Whereas sections 2, 3 and 4 seem concerned with an understanding of the wide variety of ways in which language is used in contemporary society, the 'Development' section could be more properly described as social history. Students are required to be aware of the socio-historical impact of roads, railways and canals as well as telecommunications. It is commonly rumoured amongst teachers that this section was 'tacked on' to the syllabus to lend the new subject the academic respectability which history enjoys as an established and respected area of academic enquiry.

3.53. More recent examination papers have made use of 'visuals' — i.e. diagrams, graphs, charts etc. For example, models of the communication process have been presented in flowchart form; an illustration involving stick figures appeared in the 'Means of Communication' section; and in the same section students were once asked to present information in algorithm form. A further example would be the examination question which required the student to comment on two diagrams which represented inter-personal relationships within a company, and to produce a third, alternative diagram. This parallels the increased interest in recent years concerning graphic representations, to the extent that nearly all EAP and EST (English for Science and Technology) textbooks currently being published contain a significant number of charts, diagrams, drawings and other illustrations.

Once again, English teaching to native speakers seems to be following in the footsteps of EFL — that is, it is acquiring some of the characteristics of ESP.

4. Paper 2

Whereas Paper 1 is primarily concerned with 'content', Paper 2 is an examination in the use of language. The material is presented in the form of three Case Studies. A few days before the examination itself, students are provided with sets of materials or 'realia' to study. They may then select one of the three as the material on which to answer questions.

4.1 An Example of a Case Study

One of the three case studies in the 1980 Paper 2 examination used as its 'realia' a booklet that had been produced to introduce new pupils to the workings of a school. The examinees were given a complete copy of the booklet, together with a letter to a local newspaper from a worried parent and an information sheet produced by the local development corporation. Thus the students were able to read the material thoroughly before exam day itself. On the day of the examination the students were set the following tasks:

"As a reporter on the local paper you have been asked to use the details in the booklet and information sheet to produce the following drafts:

1. a prepared set at least 10 questions in readiness for an interview with the Principal. Your hope is to elicit even more information for use in a special feature on the school that your paper is planning to do later. (25 marks)

2. a 300 word article on the advantages from the pupils' point of view of such a booklet. (30 marks)

3. a reply in the diary column of your paper commenting on the 'Worried Parent' letter. (20 marks)

4. the Principal asks for your frank assessment of the book as a piece of communication. Give your assessment in note form."

4.2 Other Case Studies

Tasks set in other case studies have included:

● write: replies to business letters
            a personal letter
            a memo
            a proposal for a photographic display
            a proposal for a videotape
            a proposal for a slide/cassette programme

a filmscript synopsis
a storyboard for an advertisement
a chairman's speech of introduction
a job description
an article for a school magazine
an article for a railway society bulletin

● prepare: interview questions
the layout of an information sheet

● design: a display advertisement
a job advertisement
a poster

● draw up: a chart

● select photos for a publicity campaign and justify the choices made.

The 'realia' in case studies has included:

articles taken from newspapers and magazines
letters to newspapers/magazines/business clients
film reviews
DHSS leaflets
a society's balance sheets
a Midland Bank guide to banking for students
a development corporation glossy brochure
a Sealink car ferry guide

4.3   Comment on Paper 2

The case study approach using authentic texts again seems a reflection of trends established some years earlier in the EFL world. The tasks are not confined to the language demands of any one particular occupation, however, but simulate the type of activity carried out in any white-collar professional occupation, or by professionals in their leisure time. If any occupational area is emphasized it is journalism or publicity, but the field is kept deliberately broad. It is therefore akin to English for Occupational Purposes (EOP) but the occupation is not so precisely specified. In this instance, Communication Studies seems to be in step with recent developments in ESP where there has been a shift away from narrowly-defined purposes (e.g. *English for Electrical Engineers, English for Mechanical Engineers* and the other titles in the Oxford University Press English in Focus Series) to a broader skills approach (e.g. *Skills for Learning*, Nelson, 1981). Whatever criticisms are made of Paper 2, and it certainly has limitations, it represents a significant shift in English teaching away from literary appreciation to 'utilitarian', practical purposes.

5. The Project

30% of the student's marks are derived from a project which he carries out. The student can choose any topic for the project, and the form in which the project is presented is also a matter of choice for the student. The examining board stipulates the following alternatives:

- a 4,000 word factual report on a current situation, project, process or test

- an instruction manual in depth, for operating and servicing a piece of equipment

- an instruction manual for carrying out a procedure or procedures

- a guide to the working of an institution or organization, or of a social or commercial service

- a television programme or film (15 minutes)

- a sound radio programme (15 minutes)

However, the syllabus also states that other valid forms of communication project will be sympathetically considered by the Board. In practice, this means that the project can take any form at all, provided the student can justify his choice of form. Thus, for example, the project might be a series of display boards on a topic for an exhibition. Examples of projects from Exeter College include:

- a set of games for teaching French language in English secondary schools

- a guide to bar coding used on packaging in supermarkets

- a report on the feasibility of a footwear wholesaler starting a retail outlet as well

- a series of leaflets describing routes for walks on Dartmoor

- a display explaining the content of A-level Communication Studies

- an instructional video to teach secondary school students how to play rugby

- a slide/cassette sequence outlining the history of the British police

- a cassette introducing tourists to points of interest in a local church

- a video advertising a place of interest to tourists

- a slide/cassette programme about advertising to be used as a teaching aid in A-level Communication Studies classes

- a booklet introducing voluntary workers to their work in a home for handicapped children

- a guide to VAT (Value Added Tax) for the self-employed

The A-level Communication Studies project is different from most school projects in that the student must demonstrate that there is a proven need for the information which he is communicating. Thus, for instance, the student who is making a slide/cassette sequence outlining the history of the police to be used as part of the exhibition in a police museum, would have to submit to the examiners a letter from the policeman in charge of the museum confirming that there is an 'information gap' in the museum, a gap which could be appropriately filled by a slide/cassette sequence. The student would also need to design a brief questionnaire to be completed by visitors to the museum to check whether visitors would be interested in such a programme. This stage is known as 'pre-testing'. Once the material has been produced, the student must then 'post-test' the project, in this case by setting up the slide/cassette sequence in the museum and checking its effectiveness (perhaps via a questionnaire or interviews) as to whether visitors bothered to watch it, what improvements they felt needed to be made, and so on.

It is not sufficient, then, for a student to embark upon a project out of intrinsic interest in the topic. Instead, he must define his or her audience very specifically, carry out a form of market research to check that there is a communication need, and after producing the project he must carry out further market research to assess the extent to which the original aim has been achieved. Finally the student is required to carry out 'self-assessment', whereby he discusses the extent to which the project succeeded and why.

5.1   Comment on the Project

5.11. The project seems to be the most innovative aspect of the A-level assessment. Whereas students are probably familiar with 'scrap-book' style projects in which information is brought together on a topic from a variety of sources, the A-level project is far more rigorous and demanding in that a need for the information has to be substantiated at every stage. As a result of the emphasis in communication for a specific purpose, the task is much more like the communication tasks performed in 'real life'. It is English for a specific purpose, rather than an exercise for its own sake.

5.12. The project is internally marked by the same person who tutors the student during the project. The tutor therefore has a difficult task. He cannot give the student too much guidance or he will end up marking what is largely his own work: yet at the same time he clearly has a responsibility to give the student some advice. Furthermore, the tutor is to an extent personally involved, in that he will have taught the student throughout a substantial part of the rest of the course. In my case I teach the students for most of their two year A-level course, act as their academic tutor for their work throughout the college, deal with any pastoral matters, and also mark their projects. Under these circumstances it would be difficult for anyone to remain entirely objective. The spread of marks is checked by an external moderator who also looks at a sample of projects and so fairly uniform standards are probably achieved, but there are difficulties in such a system.

6. Oral Examination

While 30% of a student's marks are derived from the project, this is divided into 20% for the project itself and 10% for an oral interview in which the student is questioned about the project. Marks are awarded according to the student's ability to express himself, and the extent to which the student demonstrates an awareness of the communicative effectiveness of the project.

6.1 Comment on the Oral Examination

Again the oral examination is a technique which has been in use for quite some time in EFL, but is only just being recognized as valid in the testing of native speakers, particularly for the more academically able student. The marking of the oral exam involves the same problems as marking the written project, since it is in most cases the member of staff who taught the student who interviews the student.

7. What EFL Teachers can Learn from Communication Studies

7.1 Communication Studies and EFL teaching

EFL is taught under an extremely wide range of circumstances throughout the world, and it would therefore be foolhardy to be prescriptive. However, in the smaller world of EAP (English for Academic Purposes) in recent years, publishers have produced a spate of textbooks for very specific groups of students. The parallel in teaching English to native speakers is the TEC General and Communication Studies Syllabus which concentrates exclusively on industry, and BEC courses which never look beyond the narrow confines of the office. Communication Studies has provided a timely antidote to the over-specific syllabus, and I believe EAP would benefit too from broadening its horizons in the same way, as the over-specific language course can become dull and counter-productive.

EFL teachers might also consider emulating the way in which A-level Communication Studies makes use of project work as a learning experience. Projects are an ideal way for students to apply a variety of micro-skills in a realistic, purposeful way. Project work would be especially relevant to students learning English for academic purposes, as students have to collect the information they require by using a library and/or other sources, skim through publications for relevant information, extract the details they require, synthesize the information, and present it in a concise form. In other words, the skills required for a Communications Studies project are the same as those required by most students in higher education much of the time.

A further possibility would be for EFL teachers to make greater use of communications hardware, often referred to as 'educational technology'. This has had a chequered career in EFL. For example, considerable sums of money were spent on language laboratories in the sixties, yet it is common today for teachers to say that virtually as much language practice can be achieved with one cassette recorder plus group work and pair work. Similarly there was also a vogue at one time for 'the audio-visual approach', and whole courses were based around slide/cassette sequences. Today a great deal of experimentation is under way with video discs, with some enthusiasts suggesting they will replace textbooks. However, all this equipment has been intended for use by the teacher, whereas experience of A-level Communication Studies suggests much more learning could take place by putting it in the hands of the students. For example, students would learn a great deal by writing their own slide/cassette sequences, making their own video tapes, recording interviews, mounting a display, or producing overhead projector transparencies to support an oral presentation. This type of work need not be confined to the more artistic students with a liberal arts background—visual communication in the form of graphs, charts and diagrams is central in science and engineering, and to a lesser extent is also used in the social sciences. However, although the understanding of visual communication and manipulating 'information transfer' exercises are now commonplace in EAP textbooks, students are rarely required to communicate actively in any form other than the written word. The production of audio and/or visual material by *students* could be integrated into most language courses for non-native speakers, especially those preparing students to study in English.

7.2 Communication Studies and EFL Testing

Project work could also be incorporated into EFL testing. A project is in many ways a far greater test of a student's communicative competence than many of the tasks set in more conventional EFL examinations. Clearly there could be administrative problems, and it might never be possible to use this technique on an international scale, such as that of the English Language Testing Service used by the British Council in some 80 countries overseas; but it *could* be used within the UK. It is particularly appropriate to students who are learning English for academic purposes since gathering, synthesizing and presenting information is a major part of any student's work in higher education. The present JMB Test in English (Overseas)—used for assessing a student's ability to cope with the language requirements of higher education—does not assess this aspect of a student's abilities at all. The Associated Examining Board, which devised the Communication Studies syllabus, is currently working on a test in English for academic purposes and so perhaps project work will make its way into the world of EFL testing.

8. Conclusion

Communication Studies A-level has various parallels with ESP, particularly in its focus upon the uses to which language is put. In other words, the syllabus seems to be based on some sort of intuitive needs analysis. It takes a 'wide-angle' approach, and since sixth-form students often do not have a clear career plan this would seem most appropriate. It inevitably has its weak points and limitations, but on the whole seems to be a positive step towards worthwhile English teaching for native speakers. EFL teachers might benefit from incorporating the project work approach of Communication Studies into both their teaching and testing.

Further Reading

ADAMS, A. and HOPKIN, T. *Sixth Sense: English—A Case Study*, Blackie, 1981. (Exeter College was one of the first centres to offer A-level Communication Studies when it began in 1976. In *Sixth Sense* John Needle, (Senior Lecturer in Communication Studies) gives an account of the teething problems encountered and approaches used.)

DIXON, J. *et al. Education 16 to 19* Macmillan, 1979. (The Schools Council carried out a major survey of English teaching for the 16 to 19 age group in the 1970s and Dixon gives an account of their findings, along with recommendations. The AEB A-level was largely a response to this survey.)

The booklet *Exploring a New 'A' Level: Communication Studies* was also produced by the Schools Council project team. It consists of two accounts of teaching A-level Communication Studies, one by John Needle of Exeter College and one by two teachers at Hazel Grove High School, Stockport. It can be obtained by writing to:

J. Dixon
Director of Schools Council Project English 16–19
Bretton Hall College
West Bretton
Wakefield
West Yorkshire WF4 4LG

Editor's Comment

In describing his experience of teaching the AEB's A-level Communication Studies course, David Neill spins a number of threads into ESP. For example, he puts a timely finger on the 'wide-angle' vs. 'narrow-angle' debate in ESP, and argues that ESP should move away from over-specific syllabuses. He also advocates greater use of project work in ESP. A particularly interesting suggestion in this connection is for students to produce their own audio and/or visual material as input to project-writing. This of course is part of another (wider) debate in ESP: Do we (as ESP teachers) assume too much responsibility for our students' learning? In other words, by providing too much of the input ourselves, do we actually restrict our students' capacity for *learning how to learn?* Perhaps Communication Studies, in putting on the *student's* shoulders much more responsibility for his own learning, has lessons for ESP.

RCW